RISE
FROM
WANT

1962   *The Decline of the Venetian Nobility as a Ruling Class.* Baltimore.

1970   *Pursuit of Power: Venetian Ambassadors' Reports on Spain, Turkey, and France in the Age of Philip II, 1560–1600* (editor, translator). Harper & Row.

1975   *A Venetian Family and Its Fortune, 1500–1900: The Donà and the Conservation of Their Wealth.* Philadelphia.

RISE
FROM
WANT

A Peasant Family
in the Machine Age

JAMES C. DAVIS

upp

University of Pennsylvania Press · Philadelphia · 1986

Library of Congress Cataloging-in-Publication Data
Davis, James C. (James Cushman)
Rise from want.
Bibliography: p.
Includes index.
1. Peasantry—Yugoslavia—Slovenia—Case studies.
2. Zuzek family. 3. Peasantry—Karst (Yugoslavia and
Italy) 4. Karst (Yugoslavia and Italy)—Social conditions.
5. Karst (Yugoslavia and Italy)—Economic conditions.
I. Title.
HD1536.Y8D38   1986   305.5'63   86-19228
ISBN 0-8122-8034-2

DESIGN: Adrianne Onderdonk Dudden

To my friends and colleagues

Contents

Maps, illustrations, and tables   ix
Preface   xi
Acknowledgments   xvii

1   Serfs' Niches   3

2   Bare Survival   14

3   The Waning of the Old Order   27

4   Ripple Effects   36

5   Surplus People   51

6   A Peasant in the Machine Age   64

7   Slots for Proletarians   79

8   Becoming Modern   91

9   Costs of War   107

10   Tarnished Miracle   120

Rise From Want

A Suggestion About the Larger Picture   133
Notes   135
Bibliography   153
Index   163

Maps, Illustrations, and Tables

MAPS

1. The Karst plateau area in its modern political setting   xii
2. The Žužeks' home area   5
3. Vižovlje and surrounding fields in 1819   19

ILLUSTRATIONS

1. Former Žužek house in Slivno   8
2. A Karst farmer, 1850   30
3. The castle of Duino   32
4. View of Trieste, mid-nineteenth century   38
5. Quarry near Trieste   44
6. A Karst peasant girl, about 1890   58
7. Dockside scene in Trieste, about 1890   61
8. A steam locomotive in Vižovlje, 1910   65
9. Valentin Žužek (1891–1979), while in military service   69
10. Valentin Žužek and family, 1946   75
11. Women and children of Mavhinje, early in World War I   77
12. Marija Žužek (1896–1935)   86
13. Sardine plant workers at Duino, about 1914   88
14. Vida Žužek in government-run day camp, mid-1930s   103
15. Franc Žužek in about 1940   105
16. Fire-gutted houses of Franc and Valentin Žužek, 1944   116

17. Marija Colja, midwife, taking cows to pasture   122
18. Franc Žužek at eighty-five   129

TABLES

1. Line of descent from Jurij Žužek to Franc Žužek   xiv
2. Children of Tomaž (1774–1830) and Marina (1781–1817), with recorded causes of death   22
3. Children of Matija (1801–42) and Marijana (1800–1858), with recorded causes of death   25
4. Children of Jožef[1] (1826–98) and Frančiška (1825–90), with recorded causes of death   39
5. Žužek children alive at age one and age twenty   52
6. Children of Jožef[II] (1853–1901) and Marija (1852–1928), with recorded or known causes of death   66
7. Children of Franc (1888–1978) and Lojza (1896–1976)   99

Preface

Most of our forefathers went hungry and died early. We are better fed; we are more secure; we live longer.

That change from worse to better is the subject of this book. It explores the ways in which a family of poor peasants in the Karst plateau above Trieste, Italy, experienced the effects of industrialization and modernization and lived through that great change, that rise from want.

The city of Trieste (see Map 1) is largely Italian in speech and culture, Austrian by upbringing, and an international port by nature. But one has only to take the funicular tram up the steep hills that hem in the city to arrive in another world. Here is the first stretch of the rocky and windswept Karst plateau, which rolls on and on, under different names, far down the Balkan Peninsula. Here too is the beginning of Slavic Europe. Although the border of Yugoslavia is a few miles farther inland, even here, in this Italian part of the Karst, the people speak Slovene, the language of northern Yugoslavia. They belong to the great language family of the Serbs, Croats, and Macedonians; Czechs, Slovaks, and Poles; and Bulgars, Russians, and Ukrainians.

And here on the Karst are people who can still remember life in an economy that was partly preindustrial. As recently as in the years just after World War II most of the people of the Karst lived in hamlets of twenty to thirty families. Although many of them by that time commuted to Trieste or Monfalcone to work in shops or factories, many also worked the unmechanized and inefficient little farms that their families had owned for generations.[1]

Map 1. The Karst plateau area in its modern political setting. *East of Monfalcone and Trieste lies the Karst plateau, which extends from those cities deep into Yugoslavia. Until 1918 the Karst belonged to the Austrian (Austro-Hungarian) empire. For centuries the Žužek family has lived just to the east of the castle of Duino, on what is now Italian territory.*

The subjects of this history are a Karst family named Žužek (pronounced *zhoo' zhek **). They are the human thread that this book follows in its exploration of the numerous social changes accompanying the rise from want. From as long ago as the sixteenth century, if not earlier, their ancestors were serfs of the lords of the large fief of Duino. (For a map of the Žužeks' area of the Karst, see Map 2.) Near the end of the eighteenth century the Žužeks and other serfs

---

* When a Slovene proper name first appears in this book it is usually accompanied by a phonetic transcription. Nevertheless, the reader might like to know a few basic rules of pronunciation. In Slovene, the letter *j* is pronounced like an *i* or *y*, so that Marija is simply Maria. The letter *c* is pronounced *ts*, so that Franc (Francis) is pronounced *frahnts*. The diacritical mark ˇ changes *c* to *ch*, *s* to *sh*, and *z* to *zh*. Hence the family name Žužek is pronounced *zhoo' zhek*. The letter *v* is sometimes pronounced like a *w*, so that Vižovlje, the name of the Žužeks' hamlet, is pronounced *vee' zhowl yeh*.

on the Karst were freed from serfdom, but they continued for about a century to be poor and illiterate peasants. During the past few decades they have slowly left the land. Their standard of living has greatly improved.[2] (See Table 1, on next page.)

As I have said, the forefathers of most of us who live in industrialized countries went hungry and died early. Most of our later ancestors then slowly emerged from this kind of life. In many cases, however, this emergence took place so long ago that the memory of it and the records pertaining to it are gone. In the case of the Žužeks this transformation took place recently enough so that most of the story is recoverable. Just as important, it did not happen too recently and too swiftly to follow, as in some Arabian sheikdom where the fellaheen suddenly find themselves floating on black gold, and where the change in their style of life takes place so fast that the flash can only blind the eyes. The Žužeks began the great transformation near the end of the eighteenth century, and the changes then took place in slow motion, comprehensibly, over generations.

In each chapter I discuss what happened to the Žužeks in the context of a question that is relevant to the historical experience of many millions of people. Here are a few examples. When the Žužeks were poor subsistence farmers, just how crucial was the amount of land they worked to their ability to increase and multiply? How did they view the end of serfdom, when it came, and how did it affect their ability to make a living? When industrialization and booming world trade finally began to affect the Karst, how did they change the Žužeks' living standard and the relationships between husbands, wives, and children? What changes in diet or housing or medicine enabled more of their babies to survive infancy and childhood? As more children lived to adult years, was there room for them in the industrializing economy? When did they first feel a need for more education, or for fewer children? How did they fare when a world war threw them back, as it were, into a pre-industrial economy? And how were they affected by the extraordinary prosperity of the industrialized world that began in the 1950s?

The reader may be curious about my sources of information for the history of these obscure and illiterate people. The sources certainly were not abundant. Whatever records the earlier generations of Žužeks may have owned, if any, were destroyed when their house was flattened by shells in World War I and gutted by fire in World War II. An important provincial archive in Gorizia, a town that will be familiar to readers of Hemingway's *A Farewell to Arms* as a World War I Italian army headquarters, suffered badly in that war.

TABLE 1
Line of Descent from Jurij Žužek to Franc Žužek

Jurij, alive 1578
Serf of lord of Duino on land in Slivno.

Luka, 1736–1807
Serf in Slivno. Emancipated in 1781.

Tomaž, 1774–1830
Younger son of Luka. Married Marina Gabrovic of Vižovlje and moved there. Peasant farmer.

Matija, 1801–42
Peasant farmer, with three cattle, fifteen sheep.

Jožef[1] ("Still Water"), 1826–96
Peasant farmer, carter. Freed in 1848 of payments to former lord at Duino.

Jožef[II], 1853–1901
Peasant farmer, carter. Survived by Jožef[III], who sold the house and land to Valentin; Emil, intinerant laborer; Franc (see below); Valentin, farmer; Marija, spinster.

Franc, 1888–1978
Laborer (quarries, shipyards). Children became welder, grocery clerk, hospital worker in London, housewife in the United States.

And the late Prince della Torre e Tasso, the descendant of the Žužeks' former lords, denied historians access to his archive in the castle of Duino.

Nevertheless, I found much of what I needed. In the archives of Trieste and Gorizia (despite the World War I damage), there were charters, wills, maps, police and tax records, and records of civil suits. In the Žužeks' parish church there were full and detailed registers recording nearly two centuries of the family's births, marriages, and deaths. (To protect these registers during World War II, the parish priest wrapped them in oilcloth and buried them in his vegetable garden.) And in the living members of the Žužek family, and in many acquaintances in and around their hamlet, I had good informants. (Historians should always alert their readers to their possible biases, so I will mention here that I am married to one of my Žužek informants.)

Perhaps it will be useful to some readers if I mention here a few studies of peasants and farmers which I have had particularly in mind as I investigated what happened to the Žužeks. I have been guided and influenced especially by these books, which are listed in the bibliography at the end of this book: Jerome Blum's history (1978) of the end of the Old Order in rural Europe; Beardsley, Hall, and Ward's portrait (1959) of a village in southern Honshu, Japan; Ronald Blythe's interviews (1970) with old-timers in an English village; Pierre Goubert's reconstruction (1960) of preindustrial urban and rural life in the Beauvaisis area of northern France; a couple of books by Emmanuel Le Roy Ladurie (1974 and 1979); Stephan Thernstrom's account (1964) of what happened to farm boys when they became day laborers in a New England mill town; and Irene Winner's model study (1971) of a Yugoslav village similar in many ways to the Žužeks' hamlet of Vižovlje. In fact, however, I am much indebted to all the authors cited in my bibliography, from Adamček to Zinsser, from Nice to Nasti, from Prude to Gross.

My occasional simple, even simplistic, explanations of such subjects as the Old Order or industrialization may prove annoying to some. Please understand that the book was written not only for those with a scholarly interest in its subject but for all those who have, somewhere among their ancestors, a poor peasant or two.

Acknowledgments

For their help with this book I would like to thank a considerable number of kind people in Italy and the United States. They are: Morton Benson, John Benton, Jerome Blum, Adele Brandi, Aleš Brecelj, Dante and Sebastiano Cannarella, Lynn Chestnut, Frank Conaway, Ugo Cova, Elda Davis, Alberta and Cajetan DeSouza, Richard Dunn, Stephen Fischer-Galati, Robert and Elborg Forster, Catherine Gjerdingen, David Good, Patricia Gorman, Werner Gundersheimer, Geri Higgs, Rudolf Hirsch, Ingalill Hjelm, Toussaint Hočevar, Jeremy Jackson, Max Kočjančič, Alan Kors, Milka and Stanko Kralj, Jožef Kravanja, Ivan Kretič, Lynn Lees, James Lehning, Rado Lenček, Christie Lerch, Aleš Lokar, Mia Macintosh, Elda Markuža, Jožef Markuža, Antonio Marussi, Pavle Merkù, Robert Minnich, Frank Oražem, Ivo Panjek, Edward Peters, Martha Phillips, Jože Pirjevec, Joan Plonsky, Susan Quant, Myrna Quitel, Richard Rapp, Alfred Rieber, Valerie Riley, Abramo Schmid, Lawrence Schofer, Marija and Nado Ščuka, Domenico Sella, Edward Shorter, Carol Souders-James, John Spielman, Otto Springer, Emidio Sussi, Marko Tavčar, Marta and Žitomir Terčelj, Svonko Terčon, Maria Carla Triadan, Étienne van de Walle, Joseph Velikonja, Susan Watkins, Martin Wolfe, Stanislao Žerjal, and Franc and Vida Žužek.

I would also like to thank the American Philosophical Society, the Council for International Exchange of Scholars, the University of Pennsylvania, and the University of Pennsylvania Research Foundation for grants and leaves of absence that made it possible for me to write this book.

RISE
FROM
WANT

1

Serfs' Niches

Before very recent times, most of our forefathers were farmers, and how well they fared often depended very much on the amount of land they farmed. In times when there were few of them—say, after a war or a great epidemic—and land was plentiful, they prospered and multiplied like mice in a grain bin. But when they had occupied all the available land in a given place, times usually turned bad. A few still ate well, but many ate less well than before, and some did not eat at all. Crowded and malnourished, they were easy victims for epidemic diseases. In these circumstances their increase halted; their numbers leveled off or even dropped.[1]

Thomas Malthus explained two centuries ago how the availability of land limits the human potential for increase.[2] Two decades ago Emmanuel Le Roy Ladurie gave us, in his *Peasants of Languedoc*, the classic historical study of just how land scarcity limits prosperity and population growth.[3]

In this chapter we will be looking at two families, or rather two lines of descent, that led from Jurij (*you' ree*—in English, "George") Žužek (*zhoo' zhek*) and Gregor Gabrovic (*gab' roe vits*) in the late sixteenth century to their descendants, Tomaž Žužek and Marina Gabrovic, who married each other at the end of the eighteenth century. Jurij and Gregor were serfs on a large fief on the rocky Karst plateau at the northeastern end of the Adriatic Sea.* They lived in two hamlets that were quite near each other and yet in

---

* The Karst above Trieste is a classic example of limestone country, and its name has become the generic term for similar formations everywhere. *Karst* is the German word for the area. In Slovene the name is *Kras*, which means bare and rocky land; in Italian, *Carso*.

one key respect—availability of land—quite different. What we wish to do here is to show how differences in the availability of land in these two hamlets, these two distinct niches, affected the lives of two families over generations, and particularly how it affected their ability to increase their numbers.

If the reader is to understand the nature of these niches, however, we must begin at the beginning. Where the Karst plateau now rolls for mile after rocky mile from northeastern Italy deep into Yugoslavia, there was once an expanse of ocean, whose waters were shallow and warm. Over the best part of a hundred million years, microorganisms and oysters, clams, corals, and other creatures lived and died here, and their shells settled and compacted themselves into hard layers at the bottom. Then, not far away, layers of rock began to thrust upward in giant folds and form what would become the Alps. In the process, the sea bottom in the area we are discussing rose and formed a high, wrinkled, limestone plateau.[4] For a time a river flowed across it, and hippopotamuses swam where now there is only rock and scrubby growth. Eventually, however, the river was swallowed by the rocks and began to flow through an underground passage. The climate changed. Wind, rain, and winter cold cracked and eroded the rock, leaving enough soil for extensive forests but also great fields of rock, grottoes, crevasses, dramatic bluffs, and big, teacup-shaped depressions called sinkholes.[5]

Then man arrived. First there were Old Stone Age hunters, who probably lived on the grassy plains some miles away and came here only occasionally to hunt for bear and deer in the oak forests. Archaeologists have been finding their traces in caves and sinkholes very near the villages that most concern us. Much later there were cave dwellers, who hunted and also kept sheep, pigs, goats, and oxen and farmed the rich soil in the bottoms of the sinkholes. After them there was another people, who dwelt within round stone bulwarks on the tops of the low hills. And then came the civilizing Romans, who took over the small port of Tergeste (later to be called Trieste), built a road across the Karst, erected villas and raised grapes along the edges of the seaside cliffs, and quarried the limestone and marble formed so many millions of years before when the Karst was at the bottom of the sea.[6]

Finally, in the early Middle Ages,[7] there arrived a new people from eastern Europe who spoke Slovene, a Slavic tongue. They settled in little clusters of stone houses and, much like the cave dwellers and bulwark people thousands of years before, grazed their cattle on the rocky hills. As time passed, they gradually cut much of the trees and brush for firewood and pastured their sheep and cows on what remained, so that the Karst grew bare and bleak.[8]

During the twelfth and thirteenth centuries, when these Slovenes were

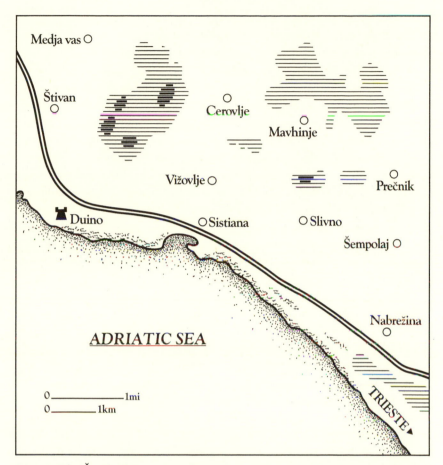

Map 2. The Žužeks' home area. *From their castle overlooking the sea, the lords of Duino ruled a fief twenty miles long and four miles wide. Only a small part of the fief is shown here. The Žužeks, subjects of this history, lived first in Slivno and then in Vižovlje. The port city of Trieste is eight miles to the southeast of Nabrežina* (nah breh zhee′ na).

probably well settled in their villages, a succession of Italian and Germanic warlords held a fortress at the edge of the Karst on the cliffs above the Adriatic Sea at Duino. (See Map 2.) From here they could prey on travelers inching their way along the rough old Roman road through the Karst,[9] and they could also force the Slovene peasants in the nearby villages to give them food, water, and firewood. But in the 1360s, Rudolf IV, the Hapsburg Duke of Austria, forced the lord of Duino to become a vassal.[10] Duino became part of the Hapsburg empire, a legacy of Rudolf, the ambitious overlord. From that time until the early twentieth century the Hapsburgs, rulers of an empire covering much of central Europe, controlled this stronghold.

From Vienna, the Hapsburgs appointed a succession of trusted German- or Italian-speaking nobles to hold the castle at Duino and defend a piece of the Karst four miles wide and twenty miles long against the Ottoman Turks and other enemies. (Other nobles ruled nearby Austrian—i.e., Hapsburg—fiefs on the Karst.) In return for this service the Hapsburgs allowed the lords of Duino to squeeze money, food, guard service, and labor out of the Slovene peasant serfs in the sixty-odd hamlets in their fief.[11] The Hapsburgs also allowed these feudal lords to exploit their lands in other ways, such as collecting tolls from merchants who carted goods along the Roman road, levying duties on the cargoes of ships that used their harbor a short distance from Duino, taxing fishermen, running a grain mill at the point where the Timavo River pours out of a grotto in the cliffs and flows into the sea, raising horses, and selling the tart wine their serfs made for them from the grapes in their vineyards.[12]

The serfs of Duino, then, were humble but vital parts of a social system in which their lord traded his military service to his ruler at Vienna in exchange for a large piece of land and the right to exploit it. Lordship (or feudalism) of this kind had long vanished from western Europe, but in central and eastern Europe it was on the rise during the sixteenth and seventeenth centuries.[13] *

In 1578 the Hapsburgs believed themselves to be in great danger from the Ottoman Empire. To cope with the Turkish threat, Archduke Charles II, the Hapsburg ruler of the area called Inner Austria, joined all of his lands into one military unit defended by a standing army. Apparently as part of this defensive effort, he issued a new charter to the lord of Duino to replace one granted eighty-four years earlier.[14]

It is this charter that provides our first glimpses of the subjects of this history. The charter spells out the general rights of the lord of Duino, and it also lists, one by one, those serfs who were expected to make special payments of money or goods to the lord in return for their use of his land. A third of the

---

* From the late Middle Ages to the emancipation of the peasants from their manorial dues in 1848 there seems to have been only one revolt by the peasants of the Duino fief. In May of 1713 they protested a new meat tax that was being collected for the Hapsburg state and probably for their lord as well. Seven thousand rebels (an improbably high number in this society of tiny hamlets) are said to have surrounded the walls of the castle. They demanded to see the imperial charter that spelled out their duties. The lord of Duino was absent, as it happened, but his commandant and hired guards fired their cannons at the rebels, killing a few and scattering the others (Bratuž et al. 1983:47).

way through the thick volume appears the name of Jurij Schuschegk of the hamlet of Slivno.[15] This man, Jurij Žužek, was almost certainly a patrilinear ancestor of the Žužeks whose story we will be following, and he is the earliest one of whom we have any trace.[16]

Slivno (*slee' u no*), the village linked with Jurij's name in the charter, was and still is a little cluster of stone houses and barns a few miles due east of Duino (see Map 2). Like so many other hamlets on the Karst, it was built on the southwestern side of a hill to escape the fierce wind, the bora, that blows across the plateau in winter. The name Slivno is probably derived from the Slovene word *sliva*, which means plum. Perhaps at some early time there were plum orchards in and around the hamlet and the farmers used the fruit to make the fiery slivovitz brandy that is so popular in this part of Europe.[17]

Why does it seem likely that this Jurij Žužek was an ancestor of Tomaž, who lived two centuries later? The name Žužek is fairly unusual in the southwestern Karst, and Jurij is the only Žužek listed in the charter of 1578 from Slivno or a hamlet near it. His name and holdings are the first listed for Slivno, and this strongly suggests that he lived in the first house one comes to as one reaches the hamlet on the road from the direction of Duino, the house which until the twentieth century was officially known as Slivno No. 1. This was the house in which the only family of Žužeks in Slivno lived at the end of the eighteenth century, the house where Tomaž Žužek was born and lived until he married and moved to Vižovlje in 1800. Houses and lands in the Karst were passed on from father to oldest son for generations, so it appears highly likely that Jurij Žužek was the ancestor of Tomaž Žužek and his descendants.

If the old stone-roofed house at No. 1 was once like the other very old ones that have survived on the Karst, it had a tall, round kitchen chimney projecting into the courtyard. The base of this chimney would have formed a small alcove off the kitchen, and here the Žužek women would have cooked over an open fire of oak or hop hornbeam sticks. The Žužeks' cattle probably slept in the other room on the first floor. Outside stairs would have led to a couple of tiny bedrooms and a hayloft on the second floor. In front of the house there would have been a cistern to hold rainwater that was led into it from the roof of the house through crude pipes of stone or wood. (This was the family's scanty water supply.[18] When worms multiplied in it, they killed them by throwing in a few pinches of salt.)[19]

In terse German, written in an antiquated Gothic script, the Duino charter of 1578 tells what Jurij was required to provide to his lord each year.[20] He paid fixed amounts of money, olive oil, firewood, wheat, rye, and vegetables. Most of these tithes went directly to feed and warm the lord's household and his livestock. The olive oil was "for the benefit of the chapel in the castle," where the serfs in the nearby hamlets probably attended mass. The oil would have been burned in the chapel lamps. The fact that he paid part of his manorial dues with olive oil suggests that Jurij worked some of the land along the coastline where the Karst slopes steeply down to the sea, several miles from Slivno.[21] This hillside, shielded from the winter winds, was planted with olive trees until late in the nineteenth century.

Jurij's payments in money, food, oil, and wood were only the beginning of what the charter states he had to do for his lord. Like all of the other serfs he also had to spend a certain number of days each year repairing his lord's roads and buildings, harvesting his grapes and olives, tending his vegetable gardens, and cutting his wood and hay. From time to time he would also have to use his own oxen and cart to haul food, water, and wood to the castle. If the lord hunted near Slivno Jurij might be obliged to beat the bushes and carry the nets used in catching hares. When the lord held his annual trade fair,

Fig. 1. Former Žužek house in Slivno. *Jurij Žužek probably lived in this stone-roofed house in 1578. Tomaž Žužek, who was almost surely Jurij's descendant, was born here in 1774 and moved from here to Vižovlje at the time of his marriage in 1800.*

which lasted six days, every hamlet had an assignment; that of Jurij and the other serfs of Slivno was to keep order. And Jurij, or some other man in his family, had to serve regular shifts of day or night guard duty at the castle or elsewhere, helping to protect this part of the Hapsburg empire from their lord's enemies, especially from Turkish raiding parties.[22]

So far as we know, there are no written traces of the lives of the succession of Žužeks stretching from Jurij in the sixteenth century to Luka in the middle of the eighteenth. Nonetheless we can make some informed guesses about them. For one thing they probably lived somewhat better than many of the other serfs. The charter of 1578 indicates that Jurij paid larger than average annual dues in money and kind to his lord, and this suggests that he had a kind of permanent lease on a larger amount of land than other serfs and therefore enjoyed a slightly higher standard of living.

Since the charter also required serfs to leave the use of their land to a single heir,[23] we can picture a succession of heirs in Slivno living in the same house for eight generations or so (from the 1570s to the 1770s), farming the same land, paying the same dues to their lord, and enjoying about the same standard of living. This would not have been a very high one. A writer who traveled through this area in the 1680s commented that the peasants lived "very modestly. They are quite happy when they have a piece of hog fat, an onion, and some tasteless bread full of bran."[24]

Of course there would have been variations in prosperity from one generation of Žužeks to another. Some may have farmed more capably than others. Some may have suffered more than others during wars, when marauding soldiers stole their cattle and grain, or from the epidemics that seem to have swept across the Karst about every decade.[25]

What stands out about the Žužeks is that as far as we can tell there were neither more nor fewer of them in Slivno at the end of the eighteenth century than at the end of the sixteenth. Just as the charter of 1578 lists only one Žužek family, so do church records of the late 1700s. The reason is clear. The Žužeks lived in a place with room for one conjugal family, and no more. Both physical geography and the social system under which they lived so decreed. The land around Slivno seems already to have been divided among the hamlet's families, so that there was no more to be had.[26] The Žužeks' small and rocky fields and pastures could feed them only as long as they did not multiply. Even if they had wished to subdivide their land, the lord of Duino's inheritance law, spelled out in the charter, would have prevented them from doing so, because the lord required that everything go to a single heir. Daughters and younger sons—those who survived childhood illnesses—must either have married and moved out or stayed at home, unneeded and perhaps unwanted, but in any case unmarried.

If the Žužeks could not increase their number in the hamlet, neither were they very likely to die out. When he reached manhood, the oldest living son, knowing he was to inherit the house and land, would have been anxious to marry and have children, both to provide himself with a small labor force and also to leave behind a son who could enjoy his own good fortune in having a house and land. His father would have favored the marriage for several reasons: to content his son, to add a woman to the family's adult labor force, and perhaps to gain a small dowry along with the daughter-in-law.[27] And the lord at Duino certainly wanted the young man to marry so that there would continue to be a Žužek who paid his manorial dues and did the required labor services. The lords of Duino are said to have made it a habit to summon unmarried young men and women serfs to the castle once a year, pair them off, and order each pair to marry.[28]

In short, then, the hamlet of Slivno provided the Žužeks with a social and economic niche in which they could survive only at the cost of keeping their numbers constant.

Now we will turn from Jurij Žužek of Slivno to look at another serf in a nearby hamlet, Gregor Gabrovic of Vižovlje. Like Jurij, Gregor was an ancestor of the later Žužeks whose story we will be following, and his hamlet is the place where they have lived from 1800 to the present day. His name too appears in the charter of 1578,[29] but his circumstances were different from Jurij's, and what we can learn about him and his descendants is strikingly different from what we know about the Žužeks.

First we must look at Gregor's hamlet. Halfway between Duino and Slivno is a low hill called Vižovlje.[30] It is at the base of this hill that the hamlet seems to have grown up during the sixteenth century. The name of the hill (and hamlet) is pronounced *vee′ zhowl yeh.* (See Map 2.) As late as the year 1494, there may have been no hamlet at the base of Vižovlje Hill. There is no mention at all of such a village in the charter that was issued to the lord of Duino in that year.[31] But eight decades later there was some kind of settlement near the hill. The charter of 1578 states that a certain Gregor Gabrovic "of Vižovlje" was obliged to pay the lord at Duino a stipulated quantity of wine each year in return for the use of one of the lord's fields. The charter mentions no other serf at Vižovlje, although it lists at least five serfs in most of the other nearby hamlets.[32] By 1578, then, a hamlet of Vižovlje existed, but apparently it was very small.

The evidence suggests that in 1494 there was no hamlet of Vižovlje but that in 1578 there was at least one family, that of Gregor Gabrovic, living there. Where did this family come from, and why did they settle in this place? We can at least offer a guess. We know that in the late fifteenth and early sixteenth centuries the Ottoman Turks and various other Muslim peoples from the Balkan Peninsula frequently raided the northern Adriatic area for slaves and other booty.[33] We also know that major epidemics swept through the Karst about every ten years. These raids and epidemics may have depopulated the Karst, leaving the lords of Duino and the rulers of nearby fiefs with too few serfs to defend their land.[34] Where could they get more?

Some of the feudal lords of the Karst are known to have brought peasants from Friuli, in northern Italy, from Croatia, and from even farther away, but in many cases they simply relocated some of their own serfs on vacant lands.[35] It seems very likely that the Duino lords encouraged such colonization and that Vižovlje was the result. This little place—smaller even than most of the nearby hamlets—is so close to Duino that one wonders if its land had served mainly as a convenient hunting ground for the lords of Duino until they decided that it was important to settle a cluster of serf families on it. Perhaps the first Gabrovic—Gregor or an ancestor of his—was settled here so that he could tend his lord's vineyards near the sea and pay most of his manorial dues in wine. Perhaps he was also expected to serve as a guard in the nearby fortress overlooking the little bay of Sistiana.[36] That there was something special about the founding of the hamlet is suggested by the fact that it is the only one for miles around that has its own common. This is a large stretch of land between Vižovlje and Duino where all the villagers could (and still may) gather wood and graze their cattle.

So the Gabrovic family may have come to the Vižovlje area in the sixteenth century as colonizing serfs. There is even a hint of this possibility in their surname. Not far from Vižovlje there were (and still are) four hamlets that all have similar names: Gabrije, Gaberje, Gabrovec, and Gabrovica. All of them probably take their name from the *gaber*, or hop hornbeam, a useful tree that is very common on the Karst.[37] Slovenes, like other Slavic peoples, are very given to nicknaming,* so we might guess that the Gabrovices came to Vižovlje from one of the nearby *gaber*-hamlets, and that somebody dubbed them with a name adapted from that of their native place.

---

* Many Karst families in effect have two surnames, an official one and a nickname regularly used in everyday life. To this day there are families in Vižovlje whose neighbors always call them "the Hills," "the Jaybirds," "the At-the-Corners," and so on, even though for official purposes they have other last names. Parish registers indicate that for a while during the nineteenth century the Žužeks were known as "the Skittish."

In any case, in the late sixteenth century Vižovlje may have consisted merely of a single family of serfs named Gabrovic. They would have had numerous obligations as serfs, but Gregor Gabrovic is mentioned in the charter of 1578 solely because of his annual payment of wine.

In the two centuries between 1578 and 1794, the Gabrovices made a remarkable adjustment to their surroundings. In 1794 the parish priest in the nearby hamlet of Mavhinje (*maow' heen yeh,* "the little village") made a census of the families in Vižovlje, Mavhinje, and Cerovlje (*tser ohwl' yeh,* "oaks") the three places that were under his spiritual authority. He recorded that there were fourteen families in Vižovlje, and of these fourteen, twelve were named Gabrovic. [38]

Putting together what we know, we can speculate about what caused this family to multiply so remarkably in these centuries. I would guess that the first Gabrovic colonist was given ample land around Vižovlje, more than one man and his wife and children could work, more than they needed to support themselves. If so, he probably left all of his sons equal shares of the land. His lord would have tolerated this violation of the primogeniture rule in order to encourage reproduction and thus have more serfs who could pay dues and guard his land.

We can imagine all the Gabrovic sons clearing their fields and pastures and heaping up the abundant rocks to make thick walls around the little fields. ("It is surprising," one of Napoleon's generals wrote in his diary after riding a horse through here in 1797, "to see how men have . . . been able to turn that land to use. . . . Carefully and laboriously they have cleared out the rocks [and used them to] make walls, [so that] pieces of land a few paces long make farm fields as big as your hand.") [39]

We can picture the early Gabrovices building their houses in a cluster at the base of the hill, marrying, and raising families. Their surviving sons, too, probably divided the land, and perhaps their sons did the same. As long as there was enough land, they probably continued to divide it up and to increase their number. In this way there would have developed a village that was also a large family. [40]

At some point, however, the Gabrovices must have found that the continual dividing up of the land was producing parcels so small that individual households could barely survive on them. As land became scarcer, life surely became harder. At this point they probably decided to halt the process of division. Younger sons henceforth would not be allowed to inherit; they would simply have to leave the village and fend for themselves. Perhaps this decision was forced upon them by the Duino lords, who did not want their serfs' holdings to become so small that they could not pay their dues of food and money. As we mentioned above, the lords of Duino required their other serfs to leave all their land to one son. They might have made an exception to this requirement in all those decades when the Gabrovices had plenty of land to divide, but eventually they would have made them follow the general rule. In either case, whether the Gabrovices changed their practice of their own free will or were forced to do so, the results would have been the same. The former Vižovlje of abundant land and an expanding, dividing family would now become a place of limits and controls, with an unvarying number of houses and fields and households. It seems likely that by 1794 the fourteen families of Vižovlje would have divided the available farmland as far as they safely could if the hamlet was to continue to be a livable environment, and all of these fourteen households would no longer be closely linked by blood relationships, even though they shared the same surname. What would bind them together now would be their physical closeness and the constant need of poor farmers for help from their neighbors.

Those, it appears, were the different paths taken by the Žužeks and the Gabrovices, two families of poor serfs on the rocky Karst. For one of them, the Žužeks, their hamlet offered them a niche in which they could survive only if they did what both the land and their lord required and maintained themselves for generations as one conjugal family and no more. For the other, the Gabrovices, the availability of land and the wishes of their lord seem to have allowed them, for a moment in time—a mere two centuries—to increase and multiply and fill their little world.

2

Bare Survival

For most people in preindustrial societies, existence was very fragile. One reason for this, as we suggested in Chapter 1, was that often the number of people in a given place had already increased to the point where there simply was not enough land to provide the food they needed. Often, too, an exploitative social system deprived them of a large share of what they produced. Food, therefore, was scarce, and many knew constant hunger. Because they were undernourished, they were also easy victims for disease. In this chapter we will examine the fragile balance between life and death and how one family coped with the constant danger of personal and family extinction.

Our story begins in 1774, when Luka Žužek, descendant of a long line of serfs in the hamlet of Slivno, and his wife had a son.[1] They named him Tomaž. The Žužeks already had another son named Martin, who as the oldest would one day inherit the family's house and land in Slivno. Because he was a younger son, Tomaž's prospects in life were not good. As his contemporary Thomas Malthus wrote, "A man who is born into a world already possessed, if he cannot get subsistence from his parents on whom he has just demand, and if the society do not want his labor, has no claim of *right* to the smallest portion of food, and, in fact, has no business to be where he is. At nature's mighty feast there is no cover [place] for him."[2]

Tomaž grew up in Slivno in years when the status of millions of central European serfs was rapidly changing. In the year 1780 the old empress Maria Theresa died, and her son Joseph, who had previously ruled with his mother, became the emperor of the Hapsburg lands. Joseph II was a passionate and single-minded reformer, and in the 1780s he issued a number of decrees that changed the lives of the serfs in all of his lands except Hungary. The most important was the "Serfdom-ending Decree" of 1781, which gave the peasants important new freedoms. Now a peasant could learn any trade or skill, marry without his lord's permission, and move away from his village whenever he wished, if he had a certificate stating that he did not owe his lord any unpaid dues or labor services.[3] Since we cannot say just how tight a grip the della Torre family at Duino had on their serfs at this time, we cannot say just what this decree meant to the Žužeks. After 1781 they were certainly no longer serfs in the sense of being bound to the land, but they were still "subjects." They continued to pay their annual dues in money, and they may have continued to perform their labor services.

In the year 1800, Tomaž married Marina Gabrovic of Vižovlje, and so it was that the two serf families discussed in Chapter 1 were joined and the line of descent that this book will follow was begun. How had this marriage come about? Certainly the count at Duino had not ordered it, since the reform of 1781 had taken control of serfs' marriages out of the hands of landowners (except Hungarian ones) in the Hapsburg empire. Perhaps Luka Žužek and Marina's father Jernej (Bartholomew) had arranged the marriage. Parents on the Karst often did this, especially if they had more lands and animals than the average farmer, or if, as in Marina's case, a girl stood to inherit most of her parents' goods. Perhaps Marina's and Tomaž's parents were closely related, since most of the people of the Karst were probably third cousins or closer.[4] It would be natural enough for related parents to arrange marriages between their children. But perhaps this young couple had decided the matter entirely by themselves. They could have met at one of the dances that Karst hamlets often held on spring and summer nights, or Marina might have been one of the women who helped the Žužeks with their June haying. Romantic love was not unknown on the Karst.[5]

At the time of her marriage, Marina, who was then nineteen, had no living brothers and only one sister, who was younger than she. It seems likely that there had been others, since when Marina was born both of her parents were in their late thirties. What could have happened to the other siblings? Probably all were dead. They may have died very young, since infant and childhood mortality in these hamlets was very high. Or perhaps they had died in the smallpox epidemics of 1795 and 1799 or in the severe famines that used to drive country people into Trieste to beg for bread.[6] In any case, Marina's parents had no living male children, and she was the elder of two sisters.

She was therefore a peasant heiress and a good catch for a younger son like Tomaž Žužek.

Tomaž, who now moved to Vižovlje, must have already known his wife's hamlet very well, since it is only a mile distant from Slivno. The hamlet where the Gabrovices had settled and multiplied in earlier centuries was now a dusty collection of about fourteen gray fieldstone houses and a few barns, huddled near the bottom of Vižovlje Hill and almost blending into the rocky slope behind them. The roofs were of tile, straw, or slabs of stone, and several of the barns were sadly in need of repair.[7] As in many hamlets of the Karst, the buildings were not laid out neatly along the sides of the road; a number of them were jammed together in no apparent order (see Map 3 and Fig. 8).[8] Each house had a walled courtyard, and between the courtyards of the houses ran narrow roads or alleys, barely wide enough for an ox cart and no doubt strewn with manure.

On the hillside above this little cluster of houses there were well-thinned woods where the farmers chopped down the scrub oaks and hop hornbeam trees when they were only as thick as a woman's wrist. Among the woodlots were rocky sheep and cow pastures whose scanty grass had been nibbled down almost to the roots. Elsewhere around the hamlet were meadows, small cultivated fields, and vineyards, all set off from each other by thick stone walls in which dangerous vipers dwelt. Here and there were deep sinkholes, and in a few places there were entire fields of nothing but bare gray limestone. A French general passing through here on the nearby Roman road in 1797 described the countryside in his diary as "very arid, all eroding rocks." An Italian businessman rode along the same road in 1800, the year of Tomaž and Marina's marriage, and wrote in his diary that he had passed "amid dark and sterile shoals of rock." And an Englishman who hiked along the same road a generation later called the area "a desert of rock" and "a stony wilderness."[9] *

At this time, as we have seen, there were about fourteen families in Vižovlje and almost all were named Gabrovic. They were poor peasants, who barely survived on what they could grow on their rocky land. A tax official reported in 1823 that the people of Vižovlje, Mavhinje, and Cerovlje were "poorly nourished, but strong, and able to bear up under the toil of the farm."[10] They must have been a drab and shabby lot: short,[11] deeply tanned by the sun, the men and boys in broad-brimmed hats and tattered woolen shirts and

---

* The German poet Rainer Maria Rilke spent the winter of 1911/12 as a guest in the castle of Duino. He wrote to a friend that he found himself depressed by "the empty Karst," which was "as inhospitable as the sea" (Peters 1960: 127). His hostess, on the other hand, loved her native heath, and in one of her letters to Rilke, Princess Thurn und Taxis writes enthusiastically of "the rocks . . . the sublime, heroic landscape" (Rilke 1958: 260).

knee breeches, the women and girls in kerchiefs and long, frayed woolen dresses and aprons, and most of them shoeless.[12] The French general wrote in his diary that the people he saw as he rode through the area "looked very wretched."[13] Probably no one in the hamlet had ever attended school for as much as a day, and what notions they had of the world outside the Karst must have been acquired mainly from the sermons of their Roman Catholic priest in Mavhinje on Sundays and holy days.

Among themselves, the people of Vižovlje spoke a Slovene dialect, one which varied in little ways from one hamlet to the next. With shopkeepers and with officials at the castle of Duino the men, at least, could probably speak a few words in the Italian dialect used in Trieste.

Tomaž and Marina began their married life in house No. 5, which had probably belonged to her father Jernej or to a deceased brother. From an inventory of Tomaž's goods at the time of his death it appears that his kitchen held a table and some chairs and stools, a tripod and chain for cooking over an open fire, pots, kettles, tableware, and two washtubs. The inventory does not mention clothes or bedroom furniture. The Žužeks probably slept on corn-shuck mattresses laid over boards on sawhorses.[14]

We can be sure that Tomaž quickly began helping Jernej, who was then fifty-five, with his farm work. Marina, too, promptly took up her duties, and those included childbearing; in September of 1801 she gave birth to their first child, a boy whom they named Matija. Marina would bear many more in the next decade and a half. After Marina's mother's death, the young couple moved in with the widowed Jernej. A few years later the old man in effect gave his son-in-law the house and land in exchange for a promise of support for the rest of his life.[15]

What kind of people were Marina and Tomaž? Of her we know almost nothing, except that she managed to endure a lot of hard work and many childbirths before her early death at the age of thirty-six. Of him too we know very little. However, a few scraps of information about his activities in the spring of 1816, when he was forty-two years old, have survived, and these dimly suggest certain traits. In March of that year, Tomaž, a neighbor, and Tomaž's son Matija walked down from Vižovlje to a field near Sistiana that was owned by Tomaž and some neighbors.[16] To their surprise they found in the field twenty-four "animals"—probably cows and sheep—that did not belong there. During the next few weeks Tomaž and the other owners of the field sought out the owners of the animals and got all but one to pay them rent for the use they had made of the field. They could not reach a settlement, however, with one Martin Colja (*tsol' ya*) of Sistiana, so three months later, on June 10, Tomaž walked from Vižovlje across the fields, past the village common, down to the old Roman road, and along it to the courtroom in the castle compound at Duino. Here he explained his and his neighbors' grievance against Martin Colja, and he convinced his lord's judge to order Colja to pay them.[17]

On the same day Tomaž also complained to the judge about his younger brother Ivan, in Slivno, who owed him a considerable sum and had disregarded a court order to settle the debt. Tomaž asked the judge to put a lien on Ivan's house, tools, and furniture to compel him to pay. Here too he was successful. The judge ordered a lien on Ivan's tools and furniture, though not on his house.[18]

If we can learn anything about Tomaž from these events, it is that he was a tough man where money was concerned and that he could persuade a judge to decide cases in his favor.

If the twentieth-century traveler could somehow return to the Vižovlje of Tomaž's time, what would impress him most would surely be the harshness of daily life. As we shall see, the farm work was grueling and endless, food was scarce, famines and epidemics frequent, life short. What seems most remarkable about the lives of Tomaž and Marina Žužek and their offspring who survived childhood is the very fact of their survival. What we shall be looking at in the balance of this chapter are the ways in which they struggled to avoid extinction.

Just how, in this preindustrial era, could Tomaž use his land to feed his family and pay what he owed each year to Raimondo della Torre, his lord at Duino? Let us, in the manner of other historians who have investigated the theory and practice of peasant farming,[19] ask what were the assets of this little family farm and how it actually worked.

The chief means by which Tomaž could make his living were the same ones that had been available to the Neolithic farmers who had lived in nearby caves thousands of years before. He could graze sheep and cattle in the rocky pastureland, and he could grow grain, hay, grapes, and a few vegetables wherever the fierce winter wind known as the bora had left a thin layer of soil over the rock.

Just how much land Tomaž farmed is not certain. He probably used what his grandson would have half a century later: sixteen acres of what was recorded at the castle of Duino as pasture, but some of which Tomaž perhaps used for crops, and twenty acres of hilly woodland.[20] For the right to use this land, Tomaž paid the della Torre family annual dues and perhaps labor services. He also had the right to pasture some animals in the village common, an arid stretch of land between Vižovlje and Duino.

In Vižovlje, Tomaž owned (or, technically, was allowed by his lord to use) his small house. He probably had a small shed as well, although it is very likely that his cattle slept in stalls on one side of the first floor of his house. From an inventory made at the time of Tomaž's death, we know that his chief farm tools were an ox cart, a plow, two pitchforks, two mattocks, three wine tubs, a hatchet, a sickle, and a flail for threshing grain.[21]

What livestock did Tomaž own? The tax collector who visited Vižovlje in 1823 reported that the people of the hamlet owned nineteen oxen ("small,

Map 3. Vižovlje and surrounding fields in 1819. *(This is a composite of two maps. "Visuliano" is Vižovlje.) Since about 1800 the Žužeks have lived on the higher side of the hamlet (the right side in this map). All around Vižovlje, dirt roads separated the large fields and pastures, each of which had its own name. "Na Rauna," for example, means "Flat Field." These in turn were divided into very small parcels. (Catasto Fondiario di Trieste, Archivio Mappe.)*

very overworked, . . . poorly fed"), twelve heifers, two calves, two horses, and ninety sheep. We could simply divide the animals by the number of families in Vižovlje and assign the mathematical average to the Žužeks. But it appears that, with respect to wealth, the Žužeks were not the average family of the hamlet. Ten years earlier, when Napoleon's troops briefly held this area, his local officials made a list of the "citizens" of the Karst villages and the taxes they paid. This list shows that three families in Vižovlje paid more than the Žužeks, two others paid the same amount, and the other seven paid less.[22] Since the taxes were probably proportionate to the amount of land owned (or used), we might guess that the Žužeks owned somewhat more land, and therefore more animals, than the average villagers, so perhaps in the early 1820s they owned about two oxen, one cow, and ten sheep. At the time of Tomaž's death in 1830 he had sixteen sheep. He probably kept a few chickens and also raised a pig each year, fattening it for slaughter in the fall.

What we know or guess about Tomaž's animals suggests that he was a typical Karst farmer—that is, both a pastoralist and a tiller of the soil, a self-sufficient farmer and the producer of a tiny surplus. He probably used his oxen partly to plow the larger fields but much more to haul cartloads of hay, water, and firewood for himself and for the della Torre family.[23] He may have allowed his family to drink the cow's milk, but more likely he sold it to a milkmaid, who in turn carried it to Trieste to sell door to door. The oxen and cow both produced dung for his grain fields.[24] The sheep provided wool for his family's clothes, but wool was probably also a cash crop. If so, his wool links Tomaž to the beginnings of the Industrial Revolution, because there was a great demand for this product in the early nineteenth century in the new woolen factories springing up in more developed places.[25] In one respect, all of the animals were cash crops because they could be sold in old age to traveling butchers, who slaughtered them and sold the meat in Trieste. But Tomaž was chiefly a subsistence farmer: his family ate most of what he grew, and he produced only the smallest of surpluses, much of which was probably needed for his annual payment to his lord in Duino. Alas, we do not know how large that payment was.

Some historians believe that peasants in preindustrial times worked only hard enough to feed themselves adequately, seeing no need to exert themselves enough to enjoy abundance or enlarge their farms or increase their livestock. In the little village of Montaillou in the foothills of the Pyrenees, as Le Roy Ladurie learned from some remarkable sources, medieval peasants took many naps, spent much of their time sitting in the sun, and took many days off.[26]

It was not so in hamlets on the Karst at the end of the eighteenth century, however. Tending sheep and cattle, making hay, spreading manure, raising garden vegetables, producing a crop or two of corn or buckwheat, chopping firewood, pruning fruit trees, tending a vineyard, making wine, gathering and pressing olives—these were tasks that went on through most of the year, and each required grueling labor from the underfed farmers.[27] A farmer might spend considerable time simply in walking from one field to another several miles away on the far side of Vižovlje or in harnessing oxen and carting a load of wood, stakes, manure, or hay. Most of the fields had to be dug with a spade, since they were too small to allow plowing with oxen. Hay grew only sparsely in the arid land, and every blade of grass had to be carefully garnered, using small sickles to cut even around the rocks and tree trunks. The family cow had to be taken to pasture in the morning, back to the barn for water and to escape the midday sun, out, and back again.

Despite all this effort, crop disasters were common. In a matter of minutes a hailstorm could ruin the fruit. When the people feared that such a storm was approaching, someone would ring the church bell at Mavhinje to drive away the clouds, and everyone would take three-legged stools from their houses and put them on the ground with the legs pointing up to break up the storm.[28] But drought was even worse. The layer of soil on the Karst is so thin that it rapidly loses its moisture. When the rains failed even briefly, the hay browned, grain did not mature,[29] apple trees aborted their fruit, corn (maize) halted its growth at knee height, and the grapes withered on the eve of the harvest.[30]

Not surprisingly, then, Karst farmers often ran out of food and starved. When this happened they left their villages to buy or beg for food where it was more plentiful. As the authorities in Trieste wrote in 1792, "The poor come, driven [from the Karst and Istria] by hunger and with faces full of misery, to get themselves a bit of bread amid the abundance; and the rule does not hold for them that every village should support its own poor, because in those places there are villages where all the inhabitants can be described as poor."[31]

As if small holdings, poor soil, and manorial dues owed to Duino were not enough, the early years of the nineteenth century were a period of great political turmoil. Between 1797 and 1813, in Napoleon's heyday, his troops brought the French Revolution to this corner of south central Europe. Count della Torre, the lord of Duino, fought for the Hapsburgs against Bonaparte, and his lands seem to have been a special target of French wrath. Three times the French armies forced their way through the Karst, sacking and looting the castle and various other della Torre buildings. On their retreat in 1813 they tried to burn down the castle, but the people of Duino put out the fire. What the French did to little hamlets like Vižovlje is not known, but they probably confiscated food, carts, and oxen, disrupted the normal buying and selling of wool and cattle, and interfered with planting and harvesting. True, they also declared the peasants' manorial obligations to the della Torre family at an end, but they imposed a tax to pay the costs of liberation. The della Torre family recovered its ancient rights after the French left.[32]

In the 1970s, Valentin Žužek, then an old man, used to relate a family story he had been told as a boy that describes the peasants' hunger in the early nineteenth century. Once, when his grandmother's grandmother was a young woman, so the story went, there was famine in the Karst.[33] Fearful that she and her husband and their children would starve to death, the young woman took what little money she could scrape together and set out on foot toward the northeast, hoping to buy food. Though she walked many miles, she never got beyond the area of famine, and she found no food to buy. Finally she returned home empty-handed to her hungry family. The fact that this anecdote, handed down for generations, is the earliest surviving scrap of oral tradition in the Žužek family suggests how large hunger once bulked in their lives.

In the struggle for survival, the children were the biggest losers. Of Marina's eleven children most died as infants. Only three survived childhood (see Table 2).

TABLE 2
Children of Tomaž (1774–1830) and Marina (1781–1817),
with Recorded Causes of Death

	DATES	RECORDED CAUSE OF DEATH
Matija	1801–42	"putrid fever" (typhoid)
Marijana [twin]	1803–03 (3 days)	"weak child"
Marijana [twin]	1803–04	"weak child"
Mihel	1805–07	"phthysis" (tuberculosis?)
Uršula	1807–08	"weakness"
Matija	1809–09 (7 days)	"ordinary"
Marija	1809–?	[adult]
Apolonija	1812–19	"swollen throat"
Uršula	1815–?	[adult]
Katarina	1816–16 (3 months)	"ordinary"
Andrej	1817–18	"consumption" (tuberculosis?)

When he recorded the cause of death of these babies, the priest at Mav-hinje could only guess at the cause. Usually he wrote "weak child," "ordi-nary," or "consumption." But we can make some guesses about the underlying causes. In the first place, Marina may have been undernourished during her pregnancies. Food was not ample, as we have seen, and it was customary for wives to stint themselves so that their husbands, who did the harder physical work, would have enough to eat.[34]

So Marina's babies may have begun life undernourished. Immediately after birth they encountered other dangers. The midwife who delivered them would have been a local farmer's wife who knew nothing about hygiene.[35] In her ignorance she could introduce a lethal infection or fail to remove one. Then we can imagine Marina trying to care for a baby that had survived its undernourished prenatal development and the midwife's ineptitude. Could Marina, who had to help Tomaž in the fields as well as tend a home, find time and strength to properly care for a baby? Her mother, who might have helped her, died only a few years after Marina's marriage. (According to the priest's notation in his death register, she died of "old age" at sixty-two.)

Dependent as the Žužeks were on the scanty rainwater in their cistern for water for themselves and their vegetable garden, how often could Marina wash the child and its swaddling clothes?[36] When the baby was a little older she may have given it a pacifier made of a knotted rag. No doubt flies crawled over the rag. Did Marina know that she should wash it?[37] Diarrhea and dysen-tery resulting from poor sanitation probably killed at least one or two of her babies. In the next three generations the Mavhinje priests attributed four Žužek children's deaths to dysentery.

Dysentery often causes a general weakness which in turn contributes to death from respiratory diseases.[38] Undernourishment and overcrowding would have made the Žužeks just the kind of human material in which the microbes of such diseases could thrive. Marina and Tomaž's fourth child, Mihel, died at the age of two of "phthysis," which could mean tuberculosis.[39] Their last child, Andrej, died at one of "consumption," which could mean bronchitis, tuberculosis, or some other disease that slowly consumed him.

How could a married couple cope with this staggeringly high rate of infant and child mortality? Historians and historical demographers have usually as-sumed that such a couple would have tried to overbalance the deaths with an even greater number of births.[40] That they would consciously have aimed at this result (with early marriage, perhaps, and frequent intercourse) is not easy to prove, since we cannot ask these long-dead parents why they had so many children. But we do know that before the "demographic transition" period, death rates and birth rates almost everywhere in Europe and North America were very high. There was certainly a good reason for high birth rates to accompany high death rates.

For the Žužeks, as for others, the only way to survive as a family was to have many children. Marina, who was herself apparently the sole survivor of a large brood, had children at the rate of one every year or two. If one looks closely at the dates of her children's births and deaths (Table 2), one can see a distinct pattern. Every time Marina had a child who survived the first few months of life, she did not have her next child for at least two years.[41] The explanation, beyond any doubt, is that she was breast-feeding her children and that when a child survived for at least a year or two, during that period breast-feeding rendered her temporarily sterile.[42] But when the child died soon after birth, as often happened, she stopped nursing, became fecund again, and promptly conceived another child. So fast did they come that in 1809 she had two babies, one born in mid-February and the other on December 30. So it went until she had borne eleven children in a period of sixteen years. She might have borne more had she not died at the age of thirty-six soon after giving birth to her last. She died during a severe famine,[43] which may have contributed to her death.

After Marina's death, Tomaž, his father-in-law Jernej, and Tomaž's five surviving children moved across the road and uphill into house No. 2, the center house in a row of three abutting ones on the upper edge of the hamlet. For the next century and a half this would be the house of the Žužeks whose lives we are following.

The struggle for survival continued. When Marina died, Tomaž's son Matija was sixteen, but his three living daughters were only eight, five, and two, and the baby Andrej was just an infant. And there was his father-in-law, Jernej, now in his early seventies, whom he was obliged to care for, and who lived on until 1822. We can imagine how difficult things must have been in this house without a woman to cook, wash, help with farm work, and look after the children. This lack may have contributed to the death of the baby a year later, and one of the girls the year after that.

But Tomaž never remarried. He was forty-three when his wife died, too old perhaps to want to marry a woman young enough for the work, or disinclined to raise more children. He would live for another thirteen years, eating and sleeping, as Jernej had done, under the same roof with the younger and the youngest generations. In 1830 he died after dictating a will in which he left all he had to his son Matija and commended "[his] soul to God and [his] body back to the black earth."[44]

The need for a woman in the house, coupled with Tomaž's age or disinclination to marry, probably explains why Tomaž's son Matija married in 1819 when—as people in the area say—he "still had milk on his teeth." He was only eighteen years old, about seven years younger than the age at which it was customary for men in the Karst to marry.[45] He chose—or there was chosen for him—a young woman named Marijana Lupinc.[46] She came from Praprot (which means "fern"), a hamlet four miles inland from Vižovlje.

Now it was this couple who had to procreate faster than death could destroy. Over the next twenty-three years Marijana had a dozen children (see Table 3). If one follows the dates of their births, from Jožef in 1820 to Apolonija in 1843, one can see that repeatedly a child who survived for a year or two delayed the birth of the next child. It was again only breast-feeding, probably, that prevented Marijana from having half again as many babies, and she continued to bear them into middle age. When her husband died she was forty-two years old and pregnant.[47]

Again, mortality was nearly a match for fertility. Of Matija and Marijana's twelve children, only four grew to maturity.[48] Their first child was born prematurely and died, and the next three died of "weakness" or "natural" causes (the priest's words) soon after birth. The fifth, Jožef[1], survived and would inherit the house and land. Two of the last seven, a girl and a boy, also survived childhood and eventually married and moved to other hamlets, but four

TABLE 3
Children of Matija (1801–42) and Marijana (1801–58),
with Recorded Causes of Death

	DATES	RECORDED CAUSE OF DEATH
Jožef	1820–20	"premature birth"
Ana	1822–22 (7 days)	"weakness"
Anton	1823?–24? (10 months)	"natural"
Mihel	1825–25 (2 days)	"weakness"
Jožef[1]	1826–98	"pneumonia"
Anton	1828–40	"scarlet fever"
Marijana	1830?–32	"ordinary"
Marijana	1833–?	[adult]
Ivan	1835–?	[adult]
Andrej	1837–39	"dysentery"
Franc	1841–42	"consumption"
Apolonija	1843–64	"hectic" (tuberculosis)

others died of scarlet fever, "ordinary" causes, dysentery, and "consumption." The last child, Apolonija, survived childhood but died at twenty-one of tuberculosis.

Altogether, the wives of Tomaž Žužek and his son Matija bore a total of twenty-three children, and of these only seven reached the age of twenty.* Only a little less than a third survived the illnesses that were then normal for childhood everywhere but that in places like Vižovlje were aggravated by poverty. Figures for only two generations in one family are hardly a good statistical sample, but for what it is worth, this low survival rate contrasts starkly with what historical demographers have learned about life in more developed and prosperous lands. In France and Sweden at this time, it was normal for nearly three-fifths of all children to reach the age of twenty.[49]

After each death in Vižovlje all of the women and most of the men would gather in the afflicted house and recite the Rosary prayers over and over through the night. How much of their time they must have spent in this way!

The Žužek family kept on going, but it was not easy, for the deck was stacked against them. They were, as we have said, basically subsistence farmers, growing food to feed themselves. Such a system is too inefficient to meet more than minimal needs. People who grow all their own food and at the same time produce most of their clothing and gather their fuel can do none of these things well enough. In addition, the Žužeks were up against a special obstacle, for their lives depended on a thin crust of red earth over the limestone bedrock. The shallowness and porosity of this layer of earth made it uncertain at all times whether there would be a grain harvest to sustain the family for another year. Also, like millions of others, they were victims of a social system that obliged them to turn over to their landlord enough of their labor and their tiny surplus of food to help maintain him in luxury and them in hunger. Finally, like all people, they were easy prey to microbes that could reproduce in their lungs, bloodstreams, and intestines and choke off their lives even before they emerged from childhood. The Žužeks, and millions like them, were especially vulnerable to disease because of their poverty.

In early October of 1842, Matija Žužek died of "putrid fever"[50] at the age of forty-one. He had been the head of a young family heavily dependent on him. Perhaps the odds against the Žužeks had never seemed more grim.

---

* One can easily understand how such terrible infant mortality could serve as the subject for Karst folk songs. In one of them a young woman stands by the shore, washing two shirts. One is her boyfriend's, the other her little brother's. She muses: "If I should lose my man / Find more I surely can. / But lose my little brother— / I'll never have another" (Merkù 1976: 36). My translation.

3

The Waning of the Old Order

On the one hand, at Vižovlje, were the Žužeks, little more than serfs, struggling to survive on thirty-six acres of rocky woodland and pasture that they
did not own. On the other hand, at Duino—or perhaps Venice, Vienna, or
their castle in Bohemia—were their lords, who were courtiers, generals, art
collectors, and the owners of a swath of land twenty miles long, four miles
wide, and dotted with some sixty hamlets.

In the first half of the nineteenth century one could find that kind of contrast almost anywhere in central and eastern Europe. A wealthy few owned
most of the land. A poor and humble many farmed it, and they paid for its use
with money, produce, labor services, or some combination of these. Many
peasants were still serfs. Others, such as the Žužeks, were now free to move
and marry as they chose. But where could they go? At least in the villages
they had niches of their own, cramped as they were. Better these than the
wide-open struggle for survival in the forbidding towns. So they stayed on the
land as their lords' subjects, paid them their dues, and perhaps longed for a
day when they would own the land they worked.

What we have described is the system or organization of premodern, preindustrial rural society that historians sometimes call the "Old Order." [1] It had
earlier vanished from western Europe, and it would soon vanish from central
and eastern Europe. It is the Žužeks' experience of that momentous change
that concerns us here. First, however, we must review what had already been
happening to them and then introduce another Žužek generation.

Tomaž Žužek, we saw, was born in the hamlet of Slivno in 1774, the son of serfs. As a little boy he witnessed an early step in the dismantling of the Old Order when Emperor Joseph II, in 1781, in effect freed the serfs in all of the Hapsburg lands except Hungary. Tomaž grew up free to marry as he pleased and even to leave the Karst, had he wished to do so. In 1800 he married Marina Gabrovic and moved to her hamlet of Vižovlje. The couple had eleven children, but only three of them, two daughters and a son, survived childhood. The two daughters who survived childhood married farmers in nearby hamlets. The son, Matija, stayed at home, married a young woman from another hamlet, and began to father a dozen children. When Tomaž died, Matija took over the family land, which belonged to the della Torre family in the castle of Duino but which his mother's ancestors had probably farmed for many generations.

Matija farmed his land and paid his manorial dues to Duino for a dozen years and then, as we saw, when he was only forty-one years old, he died of what was probably typhoid fever. Gone was the man who, day in day out, had done most of the hard physical work on the Žužek land. He left his widow, Marijana, aged forty-two, and four surviving children: Jožef[1], sixteen years old;[*] Marijana, nine; Ivan, seven; and Apolonija, who was born after her father's death. For a few years most of the work fell to the middle-aged widow and her teen-aged son, and these must have been hard times for the Žužeks.

As the oldest son, Jožef[1] of course inherited the house and the right to use his family's share of their lord's land. Now Jožef[1] had to make the lands his father had left him feed his family and pay his dues to his lord at Duino. At first his inexperience and the lack of brothers and sisters who could help must have made the task a hard one. Even in peasant family farming the supply of labor is important.[2] But in time he learned to care for the sheep and cattle and raise the crops. The fourteen families of Vižovlje were bound together by blood and godparenthood and their common need for help, and surely there were those who lent him a hand.

After a few years, moreover, a change in the family's labor supply must have eased the workload. There was a shift in what the Chinese call the ratio of hands to mouths. When he was twenty-one—younger than was customary—Jožef[1] married a second cousin, Frančiška Kobencl (*koh ben' tsl*) from nearby Mavhinje. His new wife shouldered some burdens in the house and probably some on the land as well. Then, too, as his sister Marijana and later his brother Ivan reached the age of twelve or so they must have begun to take

---

[*] Jožef[1] was the first of three Jožefs in a row to head the family. I use superscripts (I, II, and III) to distinguish them from each other.

the cattle to pasture and help with other chores. They did not go to school, of course—few went to school in the Karst until late in the century—so their labor was entirely at the family's disposal. In time Ivan would grow as strong as Jožef[1] and take his turn behind the plow, and Marijana may have tended sheep or served as village milkmaid. Only the youngest, Apolonija, was more of a burden than a help; she sickened of tuberculosis and died at the age of twenty-one.

After two generations in which they had few hands to tend the cattle, work the fields, and labor for their lord, the Žužeks now had manpower enough. When Ivan and Marijana married and left for other hamlets, another generation, the teen-aged children of Jožef[1], assumed their burdens. The Žužeks were now an extended family again, with three generations under the roof. The additions to their labor force may have raised the Žužeks' standard of living somewhat, although they could not change the basically hostile conditions that the family faced.

A hint of the personality of Jožef[1] survives in the mid-nineteenth-century pages of the parish registers in the church of Mavhinje. When Jožef[1] was married, the priest at Mavhinje wrote the usual official entry in his marriage register, but after Jožef's name he carefully penned in his nickname, "Tiha voda."[3] In the local Slovene dialect these words mean "still water," as in the proverb "Still water runs deep." Apparently his neighbors considered Jožef[1] sly or secretive.

Jožef[1] was also somewhat exceptional, it seems, for sternness toward his children. He always insisted, and harshly, that they show extreme deference to adults. When only he and Frančiška were in the house the children might speak, but if other adults entered they were required not merely to be silent but to vanish. "Out!" was the simple command. Deference to adults was indeed the rule throughout the Karst, not only in the Žužek home. It was the outward expression of the respect and submission that were natural to a society where everyone depended heavily on the skills and muscles of the adults. No head of a household could tolerate much questioning of his authority, but Jožef[1] seems to have been unusually insistent on deference.[4]

Jožef[1] was a true product of the Old Order. On the one hand, he was a poor peasant who barely supported his family by working rocky land he did not own. On the other hand, he was lucky even to have this land to use; he was the beneficiary of a grim system that rewarded him for being the oldest surviving son. And he seems to have cultivated the slyness and harshness needed for survival in his world. Such was the Žužek who would see much of the Old Order demolished.

It was a year after Jožef's and Frančiška's marriage that the great changes

Fig. 2. A Karst farmer, 1850. (By J. N. Geiger. Courtesy of the Fondazione Scaramangà, Trieste.)

began. From far-off Vienna came news that profoundly affected their lives, as it did those of at least twenty-five million peasants in the Hapsburg lands.

To understand this event, we must go back several decades. Since early in the nineteenth century, the large landholders in the Hapsburg lands had repeatedly urged the emperors, both Francis and Ferdinand, to modify the system of hereditary subjection. Why did a rich and powerful class of men who benefited from the free labor of their subjects want to change this system? The answer is that they wished to adapt to basic economic changes then under way. The central European population was growing swiftly, especially in such cities as Vienna, Prague, Buda, Pest, Graz, and Trieste. Here there were now significant numbers of business people, craftsmen, and factory workers—a great market for the landlords' grain, cattle, wool, beet sugar, and vodka. But to produce enough for this growing market at reasonable cost the landlords needed a better labor force. The peasants who were required to perform unpaid labor for them scamped on their work, and even when they did their obligatory work they used worn-out tools and their feeblest oxen. Reacting to this, landlords urged the emperors to let the peasants commute their dues and services into annual money payments or even to redeem them by paying large lump sums. The landlords calculated that they could then use the money to pay farm laborers of their own and that they would thus have a work force that was better motivated and more efficient.[5] Needless to say, millions of peasants also wanted outright ownership of the land they worked and the end of labor services.

For several decades after the defeat of Napoleon, Francis and then Ferdinand (or his councilors, since Ferdinand was often insane) would agree to no changes in the rural social order, even though they saw the advantage of having peasants pay taxes to them instead of dues to their lords. Events finally forced the issue, however. First, in 1846, there was a violent peasant rebellion in Galicia, the northeastern corner of the empire. Bands of peasants went from manor to manor slaughtering every landlord and estate official they could find. The government did not respond by decreeing reforms, and precisely by doing nothing it embittered peasants throughout the empire and helped to make them into a force to be reckoned with. Then, in March of 1848, a real revolution swept through the Hapsburg lands. The revolutionaries included professional people, students, the factory proletariat of Vienna, Hungarian nationalists, and others. The emperor now had to win the support of the prosperous peasants who held the balance of power in the new parliament, so in September he signed a decree ending hereditary subjection. His move succeeded, and the peasants backed the monarchy. Ferdinand soon ab-

Fig. 3. The castle of Duino. *(By A. Tischbein, 1842.) From the castle (the build-ing on the left) the lords of Duino administered a fief that included about sixty hamlets.*

dicated, but his successor, Francis Joseph, vigorously implemented the decree and by doing so produced a more stable social base for the regime.[6]

Rural industrialization, a peasant revolt, and a middle-class revolution had prepared the way for the great reform. It was finally brought about by rulers determined to ride out a revolution.

It must have been near the middle of September 1848 that the great news of Ferdinand's decree reached the little hamlets of the Karst. It is not hard to imagine the excitement in house No. 2 in Vižovlje. For centuries—until the 1780s—the Žužeks had been outright serfs of the counts of Duino. For the last three generations they had still been hereditary subjects of the counts. Now, amazingly, an imperial decree signed in Vienna had ended in a flash their status of legal inferiority. Even more important, the woodlands, fields, and pastures they had worked for centuries were to be their own, outright, with no more dues to pay and no more work to do for the Duino lords.

Two centuries have passed since Emperor Joseph II decreed the end of serfdom, and nearly a century and a half since Francis Joseph decreed the end of subjection and feudal dues, but people in and around Vižovlje still tell a story that seems to reflect the excitement of their emancipation and, like similar tales told elsewhere in Europe,[7] a kind of mythicized understanding of what happened. They say that the counts of Duino formerly had a "right of the first night" with young peasant women who were about to be married.

According to this story, one of the counts of Duino, generations ago, took particular pleasure in enjoying his right. If the young women were homely, he simply denied them the honor of being deflowered by their lord, but if they were pretty he exercised his privilege, and if while doing so he discovered that they were not virgins, he dropped them down a deep hole under the castle, in the sides of which were set sharp, upturned spikes. [8]

On one occasion, this local tradition runs, when this thoroughly blood-thirsty lord demanded to exercise his right with a girl he judged sufficiently pretty, her fiancé decided to cheat the lord of the pleasure of deflowering his future wife by sleeping with her himself two days before the wedding was to take place. Twenty-four hours later, when the young woman spent her obligatory night with the count, he discovered she was not a virgin and presumably dropped her down the spiked hole, because she was never seen again. The local people soon became concerned, and then angry. From the nearby villages they came to the castle of Duino and demonstrated outside the massive front gate, waving their pitchforks. Finally, the frightened count came out, and he promised never again to insist on his right of the first night. [9]

Did the counts of Duino ever really enjoy that right? Perhaps they did, or perhaps the belief that they did somehow grew out of their practice of sometimes gathering their unmarried serfs and deciding who should marry whom. [10] One can easily imagine the recollection of this usage being transmuted into a recollection of a "right of the first night." Did their serfs once riot over the murder of a pretty young girl, or is this tale a pure invention? Most likely it is a myth that these former serfs and former subjects somehow fabricated in the nineteenth century out of their hazy memories of the customs of the Duino fief and their emancipation. The myth deals with important but only dimly remembered events and enlivens them with sex, blood, and anger. It gave the descendants of humble serfs a sense that at least once they took their fate into their own hands. [11]

Satisfying as it was for the Žužeks to be freed from their legal status of subjection to the della Torre family, it must have been even sweeter to enjoy the accompanying economic reforms. No longer did Jožef[1] have to pay annual dues in money or in kind to the lords of Duino. No longer did he have to haul food, water, and wood to their castle or repair their roads or work in their fields and vineyards. And for all this he was not required, as peasants were in some other Hapsburg lands, to pay any compensation to his former lord. The peasants of the Karst officially received full title to their land in 1861.

Jožef[1] received as his own property twenty acres of rocky woodland and sixteen acres that the official records of the transfer call pasture, but that probably included some tilled fields.[12] The family now owned and could do as it pleased with land that their ancestors had been working for centuries.

The Žužeks now had all the duties and some of the rights of citizens. Even before 1848 they had paid taxes, and at some point during the nineteenth century their sons began to be obliged to undergo military training during their early twenties.[13] On the other hand, from 1848 onward the head of the household had the right to vote in elections of the communal and provincial councils. In these elections, however, his vote counted for less than that of a wealthier voter. Richer taxpayers, who of course were far fewer in number, elected a group of representatives equal in number to the group elected by the poorer taxpayers.[14]

Some of the underlying realities of the Žužeks' lives had not changed, however. If they no longer belonged to an inferior social order formally recognized as such by a legal system, they nevertheless continued to belong to an inferior and even despised social class. One particular characteristic of theirs made this inferiority especially obvious. Not only did they tend animals— and perhaps smell like them. Not only did they live apart from their betters in dusty hamlets. Not only did they wear old and shabby clothes. In addition to these things, they also spoke differently from the big landowners and the bureaucrats and the merchants in the towns. By this we do not mean simply that they spoke a peasant dialect of Italian, the common language of the area, but that they used a completely different tongue, one that set them off sharply from their superiors. Here, as in many other places in Europe, the under class was distinguished and even defined by their use of a different language.[15] Their Slovene language marked these Karst peasants almost as indelibly as darker skin color has often marked despised castes elsewhere in the world.

The life of the owners of the castle of Duino continued, of course, to be very different from that of their former serfs. By a fortunate chance, some traces of their sumptuous and aristocratic lifestyle have survived in letters written by Euphemia Ruskin, the young wife of the English art critic John Ruskin, soon after the dramatic events of 1848. The Ruskins wintered in Venice in 1849–50, and Venetian aristocratic society quickly welcomed the pretty and gregarious Effie Ruskin at its round of parties and balls.

At this time the Prince and Princess Hohenloe-Waldenbourg-Schillingsfurst, cousins of the della Torre family, were the new lords of Duino.[16] They also had a house in Venice, and there Effie met the prince and princess several times. In her letters to her mother she described him as "very amiable" and her as beautiful and gracious.[17] The prince and princess seem to have passed much of their time at balls and soirées with the great, the important, or at any rate the very rich. These included Count Joseph Radetzky, the celebrated Austrian field marshall and governor of Upper Italy; Countess Anna Esterházy, of the ancient princely Hungarian family; and the Grand Duke Constantine, younger brother of the Russian czar, who had come to Venice with a suite of fifty.

On at least four occasions Effie saw Princess Hohenloe at parties or balls and admiringly described her clothes and jewelry in letters to her mother.[18] After a carnival-season ball, for instance, she wrote that the princess was "beautifully dressed in *almost* red cord silk trimmed à la Louis XV with Mechlin Lace and her magnificent diamonds on black velvet on her head and neck. These fine ladies as you may suppose get everything direct from Paris and seem to spare no expense on their toilettes and never appear twice the same." The lord and lady of Duino had lost some of their income from manorial dues, but they were still very wealthy, and they would continue to live in a world astronomically distant from that of the Žužeks. *

Of course families like the Žužeks understood very well that if they were no longer serfs or subjects after 1848, they nevertheless continued to belong to that vast body of the poor and ignorant who counted for very little. Indeed, how could a Žužek not be humble when he watched the prince of Duino pass his ox cart in a light and graceful brougham drawn by prancing horses, while he himself plodded, just as his ancestors had done, by the side of his plodding oxen? There was no sense protesting one's lot in life, however. Was there not a local proverb that ran, "He who pisses against the wind wets his pants?"

---

* The princes of Duino would continue during the nineteenth and twentieth centuries to live a very comfortable life, traveling, spending some of their time at Duino and some in their castle in Bohemia or their villa at Sagrado or their little palace in Venice, patronizing artists, and sometimes even engaging in business. For many years before World War II they gave clothing at Christmas to all of the families in the hamlets near Duino. At present the family is far less wealthy, and the current prince has sold off much of his remaining land near the castle.

4

Ripple Effects

One day—but we do not know which day—in the mid-1850s Jožef[1] Žužek heaved some barrels onto his ox cart, hitched up his oxen, and set out for the Timavo River. There he filled the barrels with water, and then he hauled them to a place some miles away where hot and thirsty workmen were digging the bed for a railroad line that would run from Vienna, Austria's capital, to Trieste, its main southern seaport.

When Jožef[1] began hauling water not for his former lord or himself but for the railroad under construction, the Žužeks became bit players in the European drama of rapid economic growth, urbanization, modernization, and industrialization. In this chapter we shall refer to all these changes simply as *industrialization*, partly for convenience and partly because industrialization, broadly defined, really was the engine that made all the wheels turn. In these pages industrialization will mean not only the introduction of steam and machinery but will refer to changes in the whole production system. Therefore it will also involve ports and railroads, factories, skills, the division of labor within families, and much besides.

We will be asking several questions about the Žužeks' experience. How abruptly did industrialization affect their lives? How did it change the way in which they earned their livings? What did it do to the structure of the family? How did it alter their standard of living?

In recent decades, economic historians have had much to say about the abruptness with which societies have industrialized. For a while the orthodox view was that the crucial period in industrialization was usually sudden and brief: a "takeoff" or a "spurt."[1] More recently historians have been showing that industrialization often took place quite gradually and is better seen as a process than a revolution. A good illustration of this newer view, and one that is very relevant to our subject, is the recent scholarship on the industrialization of the western part of the Austro-Hungarian Empire. Historians now tend to see that process as having lasted from sometime in the first half of the nineteenth century until the outbreak of World War I.[2]

In the Žužeks' area near the head of the Adriatic Sea, the leading force in industrialization was Trieste, and on the whole the city's history fits the view of industrialization as a gradual process. Trieste first began to really boom as a seaport after the Napoleonic Wars. By the middle of the nineteenth century the city was shipping out such central European manufactures as paper, glass, and finished leather, as well as products such as beet sugar, hides, and lumber, and it was importing coal, coffee, raisins, dried figs, almonds, dates, and much more. The city streets, an Englishman wrote, were "crowded with well-dressed, well-conditioned men, the rotundity of whose proportions indicate a dark den of wares in town, and a neat snug box and hanging gardens in the environs." They moved with "go-a-head precipitation."[3]

Meanwhile the city was also developing as a manufacturing center. Its shipyards had been important even at the end of the eighteenth century. As early as 1841 the city boasted three industrial steam engines.* In 1857 Trieste was linked to Vienna by the Southern Railway, and before long other lines went in other directions. Late in the century Trieste had a large steel mill. Between 1850 and 1900 the city's population doubled, from 85,000 or 90,000 to 176,000.[4]

How did this industrialization and its consequences in the city affect the lives of peasants like the Žužeks in the hinterland?[5] Well, obviously, since the city grew and industrialized only over a long period, the effects in the hinterland were not all felt at once. The people of the Karst probably began to be aware of really significant change in about the middle of the nineteenth century.

It would not do to exaggerate, however. For the people of the Karst, industrialization was like the ripple effects of a great rock thrown into a pond. At the point where the rock falls the water erupts, and in the near vicinity

---

* Information about Trieste's commercial and industrial growth and its consequences for the hinterland is scattered through Hočevar (1965). Strangely, though, there is no good economic history of Trieste itself, despite its importance to nineteenth-century central Europe and its theoretical interest as a "free port."

waves radiate in every direction, but as the waves approach the edge of the pond they become smaller ripples. In the same way, what made high waves in the city of Trieste caused ripples in the hinterland. Industrialization, and its half-brother urbanization, created a demand on the Karst for food supplies and building stone; it gave work to underemployed farmers who could haul goods with a cart and oxen; and it led to jobs for others who could build and maintain the new railroads and graveled highways. It is with these ripple effects that we will be concerned here.

In order to understand how industrialization affected the lives of the Žužeks, we must begin by understanding in some detail just how they made their living in the late 1850s, when the transformation began visibly to change their lives. At this time, Jožef[1], the man whose neighbors called him "Still Water," and his wife Frančiška were in their early thirties. Already they had five of the nine children Frančiška would bear (see Table 4). Since the lords of Duino were just then formally turning over their lands to their former serfs (as a result of the Revolution of 1848), we have records that tell us what assets Jožef[1] had to work with.[6] He owned the house and a small shed or barn, and he now, as we saw, owned outright twenty acres of rocky hills—woodland on which he could cut his fuel—and sixteen acres of scattered small pastures, meadows, and fields, some of which could be planted in crops. He also had the right to pasture some of his animals in the village common. He owned three "bovines"—probably a pair of oxen used as draft animals and a cow—

Fig. 4. View of Trieste, mid-nineteenth century. *(Detail, by Nicholas-Marie-Joseph Chapuy and Franz Joseph Sandmann.) In the foreground are a Slovene hamlet and peasants; in the distance, the growing port and industrial center. Trieste is about ten miles from Vižovlje. (Courtesy of the Fondazione Scaramangà, Trieste.)*

TABLE 4
Children of Jožef¹ (1826—98) and Frančiška (1825—90),
with Recorded Causes of Death

	DATES	RECORDED CAUSE OF DEATH
Antonija	1848–?	[adult]
Johana	1851–?	[adult]
Jožef¹¹	1853–1901	"sudden death"
Marija	1855–57	"dysentery"
Ivan Evangelista	1858–59? (10 months)	"worms"
Franc	1859–1938	
Ivan Baptist	1861–1936	
Frančiška	1863–64? (8 months)	"dysentery"
Anton	1866–70	"pustules" (smallpox?)

and fifteen sheep. His labor force consisted of himself, his wife, his brother Ivan (until he married in 1860), his tubercular sister Apolonija (who died in 1864), and his very small children.

Like the ancient cave dwellers of the Karst and the hilltop bulwark people who lived here before the Romans conquered the area, the Žužeks and their neighbors were, above all, pastoralists. Fifteen sheep are not many; the Žužeks were hardly in the same league as the Esterházy princes of Hungary, one of whom is said to have boasted to an English landowner that he had more shepherds than the Englishman had sheep. But the routines of shepherding, watering, lambing, dipping, shearing, mating, selling the animals, and spinning their wool must have filled a large part of the Žužeks' daily lives.[7] The wool of Karst sheep was said to be "short and coarse,"[8] but Jožef¹, like his father and grandfather before him, probably sold as much as he could to buyers from Trieste and elsewhere. His wife and his daughters, Antonija and Johana, most likely spun the rest into thread to make the family's clothing. Jožef¹ would have sold some of the lambs and all of the older sheep to traveling butchers from Trieste. The sheep of the Karst, which fed not only on grass but also on wild sage, thyme, and fennel, produced a mutton that was highly esteemed in that city.[9] The Žužeks no doubt also made it a habit to sell their oxen to butchers from Trieste when they became too old to pull a heavily loaded cart. As for the cow, her milk may have been consumed at home, but perhaps Antonija or Johana or some other Vižovlje milkmaid sold it in Trieste.

On his tillable fields, Jožef¹ grew crops mainly used to feed his family and his animals.[10] He raised cabbages, potatoes, onions, beets, and four kinds of grain: corn (maize), spelt (a wheat fed to livestock), rye, and buckwheat.[11] Rye grows fairly well on the Karst's scanty soil, and with it Frančiška once a week baked her family's bread. Rye was also boiled with spelt and fed as mash to the cattle. Cornmeal was boiled into a mush called *polenta,* cut into wedge-shaped pieces, and eaten almost daily. Buckwheat also served for mush, one the Žužeks dearly loved, but Jožef[1] may have sold most of his small crop. Not far from home he kept a little vineyard, whose grapes he pressed in autumn to make wine to serve to other farmers who came and sat around his fire on winter nights. The people of the Karst love their wine. In the words of a local Slovene folk song, "For a glass of ruddy wine / A pious man will give his life / And in the grave I'll still thank God / For a glass of ruddy wine."[12]

Jožef[1] and his younger brother Ivan had much hard work to do. They plowed, sowed, reaped, and threshed the grain, and cut, cured, and stored the hay. They chopped the wood for the kitchen fire. They cleared the stones from fields and pastures and made the walls around them ever higher and thicker. They pruned the vines in the spring and picked the grapes in the fall. They tended their sheep. They raked leaves in the woods for litter for the cattle and shoveled the stalls and manured their fields. In the fall they slaughtered the pig and salted the meat.[13] The work was hardest during the growing season, but even in winter it was never lacking.

As was true almost everywhere, the women usually stayed near the house.[14] They cooked over the open fire in the kitchen chimney, washed the clothes, cleaned the house, and tended the children. They did for themselves some tasks that in more developed lands had now emerged as separate trades one paid another to do: making soap, spinning wool, grinding corn, baking bread, and stitching sandals from coils of rags. They also did the lighter farm work: feeding the pig and the chickens, milking the family cow and leading her to pasture, tending the backyard garden, cutting bundles of firewood and carrying them home on their heads.

At least three times in the yearly farm cycle, the Žužeks all worked in the fields. For one week in spring they carefully weeded and loosened the soil around the tender green shoots of young winter wheat. Peasants in fertile Friuli, to the west, did not take such pains, but on the grudging soil of the Karst it paid to do so. Then in June and again in September all Žužeks turned out for the haying. On these occasions Jožef[1], humble peasant though he was, hired a couple of migrant workers from the Alpine foothills northeast of the Karst and a flock of women from nearby hamlets. With Jožef[1] in charge, the hired men, awesome masters of the scythe, would smoothly mow the taller meadow grass. The women and children meanwhile, using small sickles and bent far over at the waist, would cut even the smallest tufts of grass around the rocks. "Come on," Frančiška would chide her littlest, "don't cry. Help. Every little bit helps." At noon they all would lunch on bread, potatoes, and water, and then return to their sickles and scythes.

That night the hired mowers would leave, but the Žužeks and the women, who were needed again next day, would have supper together. First, like most Karst families, they recited the Rosary prayers and sang a hymn. Then, with much loud talk, all ate from two common plates, using their fingers.[15] Typically Frančiška served potatoes, fruit, and "coffee" of ground roasted barley.* That night the women slept in the little barn. Next day they would all turn the hay to dry it evenly, and later they would rake it into piles, pitch it on the cart with their wooden forks, haul it back home, and pitch it up to the hayloft over the stalls.

Like ants, these poor farmers were usually in motion, and most of the time they walked. Though they did have an ox cart to haul heavy loads, the Žužeks routinely walked miles to their widely scattered fields, pastures, and woodlots. Sometimes they trudged half a day across the close-cropped pastures and austere hills to some isolated hamlet to help a kinsman with his haying and harvest. Several times yearly Jožef[1] or one of his teen-aged sons rose after midnight and walked for five hours to the livestock fairs held at Sežana or Gorizia, leading a heifer, and there sold the animal, chatted with some old friend, and then trudged back home. Sometimes Frančiška or Jožef[1] walked all the way to Gorizia or Trieste, bought a tool or some cloth, and then walked home. When their cisterns or the man-made pond in the common went dry, they carried their buckets to the seaside, half an hour away, filled them with water that trickled out of the cliffs, and carried it home to their livestock. Frančiška washed clothes at the banks of the Timavo River, a good hour's walk distant, and when she needed brushwood for kindling, she cut it in their woodlots and carried it home in a bundle on her head, even when she was many months pregnant. On Sundays and holy days they walked to church in Mavhinje, and then perhaps several miles to Praprot or Slivno or other hamlets to visit their cousins, and then home. Such was the nature of this rural economy. Sun-bronzed men and women and boys and girls were always on the dusty roads, walking, walking.

---

*Compare the meager lunch and supper provided by the Žužeks with the food farmers' wives served to their day laborers in Massachusetts in 1810: three or four rum grogs a day, a "luncheon" in midmorning, a midday meal, and a late afternoon snack of bread and butter, coffee, fruit, and fruit pie (Prude 1983: 17). There was a labor shortage in Massachusetts.

How did industrialization, in the broadest sense of the word, alter the way the Žužeks made their living? For one thing, it appears to have ended a part of their farming that they had known for generations: the raising of sheep. As late as the early 1860s, we know, Jožef[1] had a flock of fifteen sheep. Only a generation later, however, when Jožef[1] was an old man and Jožef[II] did most of the farm work, the Žužeks owned no sheep at all, nor did any neighbor in their hamlet.[16]

Several possible reasons for their abandoning sheep raising come to mind. For one thing, the emancipation from manorial dues in 1848 may have changed the options that were open to the Žužeks. As long as they were required to pay annual manorial dues to their lord, and if these were dues in kind as well as in money, they may have used some of their tillable land and a lot of their energy for sheep. If they had instead planted grains, their lord might have demanded a large share of this easily sold crop. Since we do not know what kind of dues they paid before 1848 and whether or not the lord could vary them, we simply cannot say whether the emancipation from dues would have been likely to encourage the Žužeks to abandon sheep raising.[17] If it did, why did they wait a generation before making this change?

Other explanations for their decision to stop raising sheep are more convincing. First (and this happened first), during these years Jožef[1] and his son Jožef[II] were beginning to supplement their farm income by using their ox cart to haul water and stone for railroad builders and stonecutters. Carting may have paid better than sheep raising, and they may have given up the latter so as to have time for the former. Second, the Trieste area woolen industry suffered increasingly from competition with cotton factories in the area near Gorizia. And third, toward the end of the century the European wool industry began to buy much of its raw material from Australia and Argentina. When this happened, the demand for most European wool declined and the demand for the coarse fleece of the Karst's sheep entirely disappeared.[18]

To summarize, then, by one means or another industrialization seems to have taken from the Žužeks what was not merely a livelihood but a way of life. The abandonment of sheep raising must have brought profound changes in the nature and rhythm of their lives.

As industrialization took away with one hand, however, it gave gifts with the other. For example, the slowly developing new urban and industrial economy provided ways in which country people like the Žužeks could earn small sums without even leaving their land. In their own courtyard they could pound rocks into gravel and sell it to the contractors who were improving the roads on which the developing economy depended. From time to time Jožef[1] or Jožef[11] could strip the leaves from a mulberry tree or two on their land and sell them to silkworm rearers from Friuli, who foraged through the Karst villages. And in spring and summer, Frančiška and her children could comb the woods and pastures for plants to sell to merchants and prospering townspeople: linden blossoms, which were boiled to make a tea; fennel seeds and thyme and sage leaves, used as herbs; juniper berries, whose oil was used to flavor liqueurs and gin; violets and purple cyclamens, sold in little bouquets; slender stalks of wild asparagus, welcomed in the city in the spring; and wild plants used for dyeing, which would give their hues to cloth in distant mills. But the sale of all of these earned only scanty profit.

Far more vital was the fact that the new economy offered the Žužeks ways to eke out their farm income with part-time work of a more important kind.[19] It was railroad building that gave them the first such opportunity. Family tradition holds that Jožef[1] added to his farm income in the mid-1850s by working for the company that was building the stretch of railroad to pass along the southern edge of Vižovlje. For several years he daily brought barrels of drinking water from the Timavo River by ox cart to the men who were digging and blasting a roadbed across the Karst.[20]

But perhaps it was not merely a new industry that gave him this opportunity but also that great change in social status that the Žužeks had experienced in the late eighteenth and early nineteenth centuries. If he had not been freed (as we guess he was) from labor services and other dues to the counts of Duino, Jožef[1] would probably not have had time to do this new work. This is the kind of shift in the organization of human energies that is just as essential to the industrialization process as the adding of steam power and machinery. A Jožef[1] who was made to haul the castle's water could not have hauled water for men who laid the tracks for the new railroads.[21]

And then there arose another source of off-the-farm work, in an industry of growing importance in the Karst. In Roman times, and possibly even earlier, men had quarried the fine local limestone and marble, using it for building Rome, Ravenna, and Aquileia, among other places. (Chisel grooves on some of the local quarry walls are thought to date from Roman times.) Quarrying here had later nearly vanished, but then, early in the eighteenth century, it revived. For the next hundred years the typical quarrying firm on the Karst consisted of a Slovene quarry owner and a handful of farmer/laborers who chopped out great hunks of rock and hauled them down the cliffs to the sea. Boatmen took them from there to Trieste, where masons cut and dressed them and used them to build the mansions, offices, factories, and warehouses of the growing city. Not long before the middle of the nineteenth

century, Germans and Austrians with greater capital started larger firms, no-
tably the Cave Romane (Roman Quarries), which still works its gigantic pits
near the village of Nabrežina. In the 1850s the new railroads made it possible
to quarry farther from the sea and also to send Karstian marble all the way to
Graz, Vienna, Salzburg, Prague, and Budapest.[22] Two gigantic tigers carved
from Karst marble were shipped all the way to Egypt and placed at one end of
the new Suez Canal.

It was not Jožef[I] whose life would be affected by the prospering quarries but
his oldest son, Jožef[II] (see Fig. 5). The records of the little church at Mavhinje
list Jožef[II] as an "agricolus" (farmer) or "rusticus," which he was. He was also,
however, the first of his family to earn a major part of his livelihood in industry, or at least at the margins of industry. He is also the first whose appearance
we can sketch; those who remembered him three quarters of a century after
his death described him as a tall and husky man with a full beard. In his
middle twenties he married a farmer's daughter named Marija Caharija (*tsa ha
ree' ya*), who was a year older than he. Marija had grown up in Nabrežina, a

*Fig. 5. Quarry near Trieste. (By A. Purasanta.) The woman and her daughter
have brought the neatly dressed laborer seated at the right (the head of the family) his
lunch. (Courtesy of the Fondazione Scaramangà, Trieste.)*

hamlet of farmers and quarry workers about three quarters of an hour's walk distant, which was as full of Caharijas as Vižovlje had once been of Gabrovices. Unlike her husband, Marija was of average height and wiry, the pattern on which her children would be cut. After the marriage, of course, she came to live in the Žužek home in Vižovlje.

From recollections of his fourth son, Franc, and others, we know that for many years Jožef[II] supplemented his farm income by hauling quarry stone. Twice a week he rose at dawn, hitched his oxen to his cart, drove to Nabrežina (perhaps in this way coming to know Marija), loaded blocks of marble on his cart, hauled the stone some sixteen miles to stonecutters in Italy, slept along the road, and then came home. Each such trip, which now would take two hours by car, then took the best part of two days. According to one story told in Vižovlje, it was Jožef[II]'s custom not to carry hay to feed his oxen en route. Instead he brought along a sickle and furtively cut grass in other farmers' fields along the road. Once two men caught him doing this and thrashed him.[23]

When the two Jožefs became part-time laborers on the edges of the new railroad and quarrying industries, how fundamentally did the nature of their working life change? The work itself—hauling barrels of water or blocks of stone with oxen—was nothing new for farmers used to hauling their own manure, hay, wood, and water in the same way. The two were simply spending more time doing a kind of labor that had always been a part of their work. In this respect their experience was like that of some contemporaries of theirs, southern Italian immigrants in the United States, who found employment grading streets, digging drains, and shaping railroad beds. To men accustomed to a kind of farming involving much work with a shovel, such work did not seem so strange.[24] Unlike them, however, the two Jožefs worked on their own and were paid simply by the load. They did not have to learn to obey a foreman's orders or punch a time clock. Unlike so many factory workers, they did not have to adjust to a harsh new industrial discipline that they had never known as farmers.[25]

But if the new off-the-farm work was in fact not so new and not so hard to adjust to, it may nevertheless have raised problems. How would it affect the Žužeks' division of their farming tasks? When the male head of the family was hauling water or marble, who would plow, sow, reap, and tend the cattle? That problem may have been aggravated by the fact that the stone-hauling work was available only during the warmer months of the year. The virgin marble at the bottom of the Nabrežina quarries contains water and thus could freeze in winter, cracking and ruining the stone. Hence quarrymen did their work, and still do it, during the warmer months. In the dead of winter they covered the as yet unquarried stone with earth to protect it from the cold. As a result, the quarries may have provided Jožef[II] with nearly four days of hauling work a week during the nine months or so when the farm work was heaviest.[26]

He probably had some help with the farm work from his aging father and mother, his wife, and his still unmarried younger brother Ivan Baptist, and in the last decade of his life he would have had the labor of his teen-aged sons. We cannot be sure just what divisions of labor were made, but we can be certain that in one way or another the head of this household must have shifted some of his farm work, his own traditional burden, to the shoulders of others.

But what would happen to the position of Jožef[II] as family head when he was often away from home, when his wife and children did more of the farming, when he, therefore, could give them fewer orders, and when his strength and skills seemed less required? Would such changes not have shrunk his authority within the family?[27]

Historians who have studied changes in power in families have usually studied those who moved from the farm to the town and the factory, not farm families who stayed on the land. These historians have usually guessed from the scanty evidence that their urbanizing families became more "democratic."[28] But what about the Žužeks, who stayed on the land but also felt the ripple effects of industrialization?

There are at least some hints that there was indeed some democratization of the family. According to his fourth son, Franc, Jožef[II] was less firm in his demand that children be silent in the presence of adults than his father Jožef[I] (Franc's grandfather) had been. In addition, the wife of Jožef[II], Marija, seems to have developed an aggressive personality and a sharp tongue. As we shall see, after her husband's death she would to some degree control and subjugate her oldest son, a grown man. Would she have developed in this way if her husband's work had not kept him away so much? Any time and place, presumably, can produce sharp-tongued people of either sex, but perhaps economic changes allowed Marija Žužek a new role in her family and an assertive style of behavior.

How did industrialization affect the Žužeks' standard of living? Did it, at least at first, impoverish them and force them down into a growing rural proletariat? Marxist historians, and others too, have often claimed that industrialization, carried out by private investors and managers, inevitably did just that. Other historians admit that the initial decades of industrialization were harsh, especially for the factory workers, but they also claim that fairly soon industrialization usually brought about a general rise in real income.[29] In the case of the Žužeks, a small measure of prosperity did indeed, like the water that made its way out of the seaside cliffs at Sistiana, trickle down.

Back at the beginning of the nineteenth century, the life of the Žužeks, as we saw, was harsh. Only three of the eleven children born to Tomaž and Marina Žužek in the very early 1800s had reached maturity. The family ate only what they could produce on their own stony land, and only after deducting from that what they had to pay to their lord at Duino. We remember the tax collector's description of the "poorly nourished" people of Vižovlje and nearby hamlets, and their "weary" beasts.

By the end of the nineteenth century their life was still hard, but the economic quickening had clearly raised the Žužeks' standard of living. For one thing, they had probably improved their house. It seems best merely to summarize how this is likely to have happened.[30] At the start of the nineteenth century, theirs was probably the typical old-style Karst farmhouse: two floors topped by a steep roof of flat fieldstones,[31] a fat kitchen chimney projecting into the courtyard in front of the house, a kitchen and cattle stalls on the first floor, a hayloft and two small, dark bedrooms on the second. It was probably much like the old Žužek house in Slivno (see Fig. 1).

Several things probably enabled the Žužeks to improve their house during the nineteenth century: their own very modest gains in prosperity, especially after 1860 or so; the rise of industries producing building materials across the border in Italy; and the growth of building and stonecutting skills on the Karst. On some momentous day the Žužeks must have decided on a major home improvement. They would have driven their ox cart into Italy a number of times and purchased enough manufactured red tiles to cover the roof. After they had carted them home they would have thrown off the fieldstones and removed the rafters. Then, with the help of a mason, they would have built the front and rear walls of the house about four feet higher (the use of tiles would have made this feasible because they require a less steep pitch than do fieldstones), replaced the rafters, and covered them with tiles. They would now have had a better roof and, what is more important, a third floor.[32]

During the latter half of the nineteenth century, the Žužeks built a small stone cattle barn on the right-hand side of the courtyard in front of the house.[33] This would have allowed them to convert the first-floor cattle stalls and the second-floor hayloft into living space. Adding a third floor and removing the cattle to a barn must have approximately doubled their living space and perhaps raised the level of hygiene as well.

Meanwhile, the fact that there were now local men trained in the quarries to cut stone probably made it possible to improve the house in other ways. Like other families on the Karst, in these decades the Žužeks may have paid stonecutters to make them large stone lintels so that they could enlarge their tiny, square window openings and use in them the larger panes of glass that they could now purchase. Perhaps they built themselves a large cistern, with stone pipes to carry water to it from their roof. And perhaps they added the usual stone lintel over the gateway to their courtyard, inscribed with their name and the year and the letters IHS (short for the Greek form of the word *Jesus*). But we may only say "perhaps," because the evidence of such changes was later destroyed in World War I when Vižovlje was shelled and leveled.

Not only were the Žužeks probably better housed by the end of the century; they also were very likely better fed. By the second half of the century, famines were a thing of the past. Improved roads, the new railroads, and Trieste's vigor as a port all made it virtually impossible to have a local food shortage that could not be relieved by imports, and with his added income from stone carting, Jožef[11] could now have bought at least some of his family's food, supplementing what he grew.

The Žužeks' food was simple, however. At the end of the century (Franc Žužek would recall as an old man), they usually ate dark bread, cornmeal mush or potatoes, and whatever vegetables the garden was producing, such as turnips, beets, cabbages, or beans. In the spring the older children might gather wild asparagus or elderberry blossoms, and their mother would fry them in a batter made of egg and flour. Their cow provided at least some milk for the children, and the adults drank sparingly of their homemade wine, a mild and cloudy white and a vinegary red. (People of the Karst consider the red particularly nourishing; it "makes blood.")[34] On rare holidays they might eat one of their chickens, but like most European country people they ate little meat.[35] If a woman was observed by her neighbors to be cooking beef, they would ask, "Who's sick?" on the assumption that no one would spend money so lavishly except to nourish an invalid. Rarely, the adults—but not the children—might have some sausage or ham. Despite the nearness of the sea, they almost never ate fish.

By comparison, white Americans in the second half of the nineteenth century, who were still predominantly country people like the Žužeks, may have eaten less fruit and vegetables, but they probably ate more wheat and considerably more meat and milk. Even American black slaves, on the eve of the Civil War, probably ate more meat than the Žužeks, although in general their diet was less nutritious.[36]

Although the Žužeks' diet was monotonous and seems to have been short on fats and protein, we suspect, as we said, that the Žužeks were now better fed than their great-grandparents. Franc Žužek's recollection was that he was seldom really hungry as a boy in about 1900. There was enough to eat, even if the spectrum of available foods was narrow. Some of his contemporaries, however, recall real, gnawing hunger. One of them stated that he believed it was hunger that often, when he was a child, made adults and children alike irrational and fearful of spirits and the dark.[37]

As for clothing, it is likely that by the end of the century the Žužeks were somewhat better dressed than they had been earlier. Since they no longer owned sheep, they would no longer have been dressed in clothes made of their own homespun woolen cloth. But one of the triumphs of the Industrial Revolution was the manufacture of woolen and cotton cloth that even the poor could afford to buy. With the small income that Jožef[II] made by hauling stone, they probably bought material on rare occasions and had a nearby tailor make their clothes. Even so, their clothes were still few and much worn. As Franc Žužek recalled much later, the children wore the adults' hand-me-downs until Marija could no longer stitch and patch them together. On their feet the adults often wore sandals made by coiling rags and sewing them to form soles. Children went barefoot much of the time, cheerfully no doubt, though their feet were pocked with sores that developed when cuts became infected from walking in manure.

Such was the life of the Žužeks who lived through the beginnings of the industrialization process, who felt the first ripples of it make their way across the Karst. Old Jožef[I] and his wife Frančiška, who had been born subjects of the lords of Duino, lived until the 1890s. By this time their son Jožef[II] was also hauling stone; their daughter-in-law Marija was doing the cooking, the washing, and the lighter farm work. The middle-aged couple had probably agreed to look after the old one as a condition of the younger Jožef's eventually inheriting the house and land, but they probably also did it because in this society, as in most poor ones, children learned early that it would be their sacred duty to look after their parents in their old age.[38] For the same reasons, Tomaž Žužek had looked after or at least lived with his father-in-law in the early 1800s, long after his wife had died; and Matija had sheltered Tomaž; and Jožef[I] and Frančiška had looked after the widowed mother of Jožef[I] until her death. This was the social security system of a preindustrial society. For those who had been fortunate enough to inherit land and who therefore controlled its disposition in old age, the system worked very well. Frančiška reached the age of sixty-five and then died in 1890 of an illness that the parish priest recorded as "dropsy." Jožef[I] lived on for another eight years and then died of pneumonia.

As for their son Jožef[II]—the tall, husky, bearded man who had been, even more than his father, a figure bridging the old semi-subsistence farming and the new era of early industrialization—he died the death of a country laborer. Indeed, what was best remembered about his life, long after it was over, was the way he took his leave of it. On a warm evening in June of 1901 Jožef[II] was sitting with friends under the grape arbor in front of the Blažina family's little tavern, a stone's throw from his home. A few steps away, in the shadows where he could hear but not be noticed, was the Blažinas' seven-year-old son, Ivan. During a lull in the men's conversation they heard the hooting of an owl. In Vižovlje, as in many other places, it was believed that the mournful hooting of an owl foretells a death.[*] Ivan, who remembered the incident very well as an old man, heard Jožef[II] tell the other men, "He's calling for me." He was then forty-eight years old. One morning soon after this Jožef[II] hitched his oxen to their yoke and set out on his regular twice-weekly stone-hauling trip. He loaded a block of marble on his cart in Nabrežina and hauled it from there to the stonecutters across the border in Italy. At some point during the return trip he suffered a heart attack or stroke. The oxen knew the way home, and eventually they arrived in Vižovlje pulling the cart, with Jožef[II]'s dead body sprawled on the floor.

[*] "It was the owl that shriek'd, the fatal bellman, / Which gives the stern'st good-night" (Shakespeare, *Macbeth*, II, ii, 4).

5

Surplus People

While the Žužeks were adjusting to the ripple effects of industrialization, they were also undergoing another slow, profound kind of change. In each generation, more of their children were surviving infancy and childhood. If we look at the experience of five generations of Žužeks, we see the pattern revealed in Table 5. In each generation, a larger proportion of the children was surviving infancy and reaching the age of twenty. Only about half of Tomaž and Marina's children lived even to the age of one, but in the following generations the proportion kept improving until all of Franc's children survived to that age. Although only three of Tomaž's eleven children reached age twenty, all but one of Franc's reached their adult years.

These growing numbers of surviving Žužek children reflect a vast social change. All over the industrialized world, man was winning a war against early death. Children who in earlier times would have died young were surviving infancy, surviving childhood, reaching their twenties, producing children of their own, and thus causing dramatic increases in population. The reasons for the widespread decline in infant and childhood mortality are still somewhat mysterious. More and better food surely played a role. So did better housing, cleaner water, and a slowly growing awareness of the need for cleanliness. Before the early twentieth century these things counted for more than doctors and medicines.[1]

Our concern here, however, is not with Europe as a whole but only with the reasons why more Žužeks were surviving childhood. In order to suggest

TABLE 5
Žužek Children Alive at Age 1 and Age 20

PARENTS, YEAR OF MARRIAGE	CHILDREN ALIVE AT 1	CHILDREN ALIVE AT 20
Tomaž, Marina (1800)	6 out of 11 (55%)	3 out of 11 (27%)
Matija, Marijana (1819)	8 out of 12 (67%)	4 out of 12 (33%)
Jožef[1], Frančiška (1847)	7 out of 9 (77%)	5 out of 9 (55%)
Jožef[II], Marija (1879)	7 out of 8 (87%)	5 out of 8 (62%)
Franc, Lojza (1922)	5 out of 5 (100%)	4 out of 5 (80%)

some of the reasons, we must first recall what kinds of changes in their manner of living took place during the nineteenth century. In the preceding chapter we saw that when they stopped raising sheep they were able to use more of their land for raising food crops. Like other Karst farmers, they probably began to grow more potatoes, and these would have provided dependable additions to their diet. Also, when Jožef[1] and his son Jožef[II] began to haul water and stone with their ox cart, they had more disposable income and apparently used this income to add a third floor to their house and to build a small barn for the cattle, which had previously shared the first floor of the house with them.[2]

We also suggested that because of the quarry industry in Nabrežina there were now skilled stonecutters on the Karst, whom the Žužeks could have paid to make larger windows and stone rain gutters that would lead more rainwater from their roofs to a new, larger cistern. And it seems likely that when they ceased to raise sheep, the Žužeks stopped wearing woolen homespun and began to buy washable linen or cotton cloth to have made into clothes.

It seems likely that during the nineteenth century a number of such changes in the way the Žužeks lived made it a little less likely that their children would die of malnutrition and disease. With more food available, even if it was mainly bread and potatoes and cornmeal mush, the children must have had better prenatal nutrition and more to eat in the crucially important early years.[3] With more water available and with clothes made of materials that were easier to wash, their mothers could keep them cleaner. As a result they (especially infants) probably suffered less from diarrhea and other gastrointestinal diseases, and they therefore would have more easily absorbed the nutrients in their food.[4] Since the family's living quarters were not as crowded and poorly ventilated as in former times, the children were probably a little less likely to catch lice-carried diseases such as typhus or contagious ones such as pulmonary tuberculosis.

The Žužeks may also have begun to understand the importance of sanitation. To give an example, it was in mid-nineteenth-century Vienna that Ignaz Semmelweiss began to prove that puerperal (childbed) fever was an infection and that obstetricians and midwives could avoid spreading the disease and save lives by carefully washing their hands before and after delivering babies. It was only after some decades that even his peers in Vienna accepted his teachings, but surely his ideas eventually reached even an obscure hamlet like Vižovlje on the other side of the Alps. At some point the local midwife no doubt learned that she should wash her hands before delivering babies.[5] There is also no doubt that a general awareness of the importance of cleanliness eventually reached all families in Vižovlje and that they began to wash themselves and their clothing more often, to shovel up the manure in their courtyards, and to wash their cows' udders before they milked them. But who can say just when such changes began or how they affected mortality rates?[6]

Medical science in the stricter sense—doctors, hospitals, injections, medicines—probably could not have affected the survival rate of the Žužeks at all until well into the twentieth century. Not until about 1900 was there a doctor in a nearby village, and even then most Karst families could not afford his services or the medicines he would have prescribed.[7] The lack of medical care is obvious in the cases of two of Jožef[1]'s children, one of whom died of "worms" and the other of "pustules," which probably means smallpox. It is likely that a doctor could have prevented both deaths. Even in the second half of the nineteenth century, when doctors had few miracle drugs available to them, they could kill or purge roundworms[8] and vaccinate for smallpox.

The remarkable fact is that even without drugs and doctors more Žužek children were surviving in each generation, and their survival raises this question: How would the larger number of Žužeks support themselves? Let us consider what had happened in the earlier generations. Of Tomaž Žužek's eleven children, only three survived childhood. What did they do for a living? Matija inherited the house and land, and his sisters Marija and Uršula married young farmers in other villages. In the next generation, four of Matija's children survived childhood, but one of them died at twenty-one, so that there were only three who had to find places for themselves. The oldest son, Jožef[1], inherited the house and land; Marijana married a farmer in Mavhinje; and Ivan married a farmer's daughter in another hamlet and moved there. In these two generations there were few children who survived childhood, and they managed to find places for themselves in the Karst economy.

It may have been easy to do this in a community where other families also had few children who survived childhood. There must have been a rough equivalence between the number of farms and the numbers of potential farmers and farmers' wives.

In the generations to come, however, as we have seen with the Žužeks, more and more children survived and grew to adulthood. The traditional subsistence economy of the Karst could never have supported them, but now that economy itself was in transition, and industrialization was slowly transforming the lives of the people of the Karst. Could the Industrial Revolution provide enough livings for the products of the revolution against early death?

It may have been in the 1870s, among the four brothers and sisters of Jožef[II], that the problem of the survival of surplus children first arose as a serious concern. The second Jožef's two sisters, Antonija and Johana, as we have seen, married farmers in nearby villages when they were twenty and twenty-one years old respectively, so they do not seem to have had trouble finding places for themselves in the rural economy. A brother, Franc, married a farmer's daughter in Vižovlje, somehow bought a house and land in Mavhinje, and farmed there for the remainder of his life. But what happened to the youngest brother, Ivan Baptist, is another story. Since he was the youngest of three sons, with a prolific oldest brother, there was not the slightest chance of Ivan Baptist's ever inheriting the family house and land. He might have married a peasant heiress and farmed her family's land, but as more children began to survive childhood, families with no sons to inherit the houses and lands probably became rare, making peasant heiresses unusual. It may have been hard for Ivan Baptist to find a wife with land of her own, and perhaps farming was not to his taste.

In any case, Ivan Baptist became a low-paid laborer in the stone quarries at Nabrežina, making himself the first Žužek to earn his living almost entirely as what we might call an industrial laborer. He continued, as long as he was a bachelor, to live in house No. 2 in Vižovlje with his father, his brother and sister-in-law, and their children.

Ivan Baptist had a streak of whimsy and eccentricity. Perhaps out of some vague awareness of the passing of the Old Order, he liked to play at playing the aristocrat. Out of his meager earnings he somehow bought himself an elegant white suit—probably a gentleman's castoff. One evening he walked to a dance in a distant village and met and charmed the daughter of a local landlord. He claimed to be a wealthy man himself, and the girl's parents, attracted by the possibility of such a son-in-law, made much of him. After the dance they had their hired man drive him home to his "estate." As the coach neared Vižovlje, Ivan Baptist told the driver to stop so that he might relieve himself.

He slipped off through the bushes and across the fields toward home, laughing as he heard the worried coachman cry out "Sir! Where are you? Sir! Are you all right?" [9]

Working as a full-time laborer did not make Ivan Baptist a rich man, but this new way of earning a livelihood did free him of many of the concerns of his farmer ancestors. Among other things, it meant that he was more free to choose a wife without worrying about whether she could bring a dowry of land. The sensational events of his first love affair make that very clear. Ivan Baptist fell in love with a girl of the Lokazu family in Mavhinje. She was no peasant heiress but one of several children, and she worked as a milkmaid. (This was poorly paid work, for which only young, unmarried women had the time and energy.) She had been engaged for the past three years to a man named Kastelc, but she threw him over for Ivan Baptist.

This seems to have been a love match pure and simple, since neither of the two young people was to inherit land. When the wedding date was near, the priest announced the banns. Kastelc, distraught and dangerous, walked through Mavhinje, Vižovlje, and other nearby villages chanting over and over, "The banns have been said, but the marriage will not be." Early one morning the Lokazu girl and five others started toward Trieste, carrying their milk cans on their heads. As they walked down the country road in the near darkness, Kastelc suddenly jumped out from behind some bushes and stabbed the girl to death. The other girls fled, and Kastelc killed himself not far away by jumping into a deep crevasse. [10]

This story has its own sensational interest, but it also makes this point: Ivan Baptist, a laborer, seems not to have been involved in a marriage market ruled by economic concerns. Romantic passion, not dowries of land or cows, motivated the actors in this melodrama. [11]

Eventually Ivan Baptist married a peasant girl from the hamlet of Šempolaj (*shem poh lie'*, St. Pelagius). Just as one might expect, she too was not a peasant heiress with a house and land of her own. She probably brought him no dowry at all. He bought himself a very small house in Vižovlje, in which he would remain for the rest of his life. When his wife later died, he remarried, this time choosing a young woman from the fishing hamlet of Križ (*kreezh*, Holy Cross). She too brought him no land, and probably no money or cattle. The people of Vižovlje nicknamed Ivan Baptist's family the "Kržankni" or "Crossers," in honor of his wife's hamlet, and the name still sticks to his descendants a century later. Much to his two wives' disgust, Ivan Baptist continued all his life to mention his first love, the murdered milkmaid of Mavhinje, when he recited his prayers by his bedside each night.

As a landless laborer, Ivan Baptist was much poorer than his older brother

Jožef[11]. He and his first and then his second wife lived with their children in a house consisting of a kitchen, one bedroom, and an attached cowshed that could be reached only through the kitchen. Twice a day his wife led their cow from the shed to the communal pasture and back, each time maneuvering her past the kitchen stove and table. Even in Vižovlje, where men and beasts lived in great proximity, this was considered a primitive arrangement.

And yet Ivan Baptist, poor though he was, kept up his mock-aristocratic whimsy. On his miserable pay, family tradition maintains, he somehow kept two servants (cronies, perhaps, going along with a standing joke?) and often dressed in that worn and much-repaired white suit. He grew a long, narrow beard. Perhaps his position as a laborer, a man not intimately involved in the traditional farming structure of the hamlet, permitted him an eccentricity not allowed to others.

Ivan Baptist's case illustrates how a young man who was part of the human surplus produced by the decline in mortality could make his way. He found work helping to meet the need for building materials in the growing cities, married outside the farm economy, and adopted a personal style unlike that of his conventional fellow villagers.

Among the young Žužek women in the late nineteenth or early twentieth centuries there was no one whose situation was quite like that of Ivan Baptist. That is, there was no girl obliged because of the growing number of boys and girls surviving childhood to find any role in life other than the traditional one of becoming a farmer's wife in a small village. Ivan Baptist's two sisters, Antonija and Johana, had in fact taken just that customary course, one going to live in a farmhouse virtually in the shadow of the castle of Duino, and the other going to the obscure hamlet of Brje (*ber' yeh*), about eight miles due east of Vižovlje. But they were a decade and more older than Ivan Baptist and may have found their farmer husbands before the great decline in mortality began to produce a large crowd of survivors.

Living in the farmhouse attached to No. 2 on the southeast side, however, was a handsome young woman whose early life seems to show how some young women in the Karst were responding to the challenges and opportunities resulting from industrialization and the decline in mortality. Since she was a neighbor and close friend of the Žužeks, Karlina Klarič's story was very familiar to them.[12] She had been born to a farm family in Opatje Selo ("Abbey Village"), a hamlet about six miles to the northwest of Vižovlje. Since she had three brothers and four sisters, we may perhaps regard her as a product of the decline in mortality, a surplus person. That is, she may have been someone who, a generation or two earlier, would either have died or, if she had lived, have been an only child and a peasant heiress.[13] Instead, because she had a living brother, she had no chance of inheriting the family house and land.

How would such a young woman in a society just beginning to feel the reverberations of industrialization and urbanization earn her keep? In her generation, in about the year 1900, there were almost no paying jobs within reach of her village. Perhaps the only way to earn money was the way Karlina chose: to carry her family's and other farmers' milk to Trieste and there sell it. This was work that young women on the Karst had probably done for several generations, but the number of milkmaids had surely risen during the past half century as the population of Trieste had doubled. This was one of the ways in which urbanization was providing work for the countryside's new surplus people.

Family tradition maintains that Karlina carried milk to Trieste every day, but this would have meant a round trip of about thirty-seven miles on foot. Perhaps she carried it only a few miles to a railroad station and there took the train to the city. If she followed the routine of other milkmaids, she got up each day while it was still dark, dressed, and put her sandals on her head, a coiled-up rag on top of them, and a bucket of milk on top of the rag. Then she set out for the city (or the train station), joining other milkmaids from her own and other hamlets en route. She walked barefoot on the dirt roads of the Karst, but when she reached the station or the city she put on her sandals. In Trieste she walked from door to door, selling small quantities of milk to housewives. Later in the day she started for home. If she was lucky she might coax a farmer headed the same way to give her a ride on his ox cart.[14]

It was all very well for Karlina to serve as a milkmaid while still in her late teens, but in her generation almost the only way a woman on the Karst could support herself for a lifetime was as a farm wife. Marriages were of great economic importance not only to the young but to their families. As a result there was a strong tradition of family-arranged marriages.

When she was about twenty years old, Karlina's father decided that she should marry a middle-aged farmer from a nearby hamlet. Apparently, even in a generation swelled by surplus people, a place as farm wife could be found for an attractive girl. Karlina was accustomed to obeying her father, a strong-willed man, but she hated the thought of marrying this particular man, and she made her objections clear. At village festivals she refused to dance with him, and when her brother took her to the town of Gorizia to buy material for her wedding dress, she insisted on buying black cloth, rather than the gray or beige that was customary for wedding dresses in the Karst. Even when the

Fig. 6. A Karst peasant girl, about 1890. (*Die österreichisch-ungarische Monarchie* [1886–1902: vol. 10, p. 153].)

priest of Opatje Selo pronounced the banns, she continued to refuse to give in. Meanwhile her parents, and particularly her mother, were more understanding than they pretended to be. A week or two before the wedding date Karlina overheard them discussing the marriage. Her father finally agreed with her mother that if Karlina continued for a few days longer to object, he would not insist on it. The girl decided to make her refusal as clear as possible and ran away to a relative in Trieste. When the parish priest learned of her objection to the marriage and her flight to Trieste, he told her parents that he could not marry her to a man she did not want, and the engagement was broken off.

We can well imagine that her father now decided that he would make no more effort to find Karlina a husband among the farmers of Opatje Selo. She could find her own husband on the open marriage market. And so she did. In June of 1896 she went with her family to cut hay on a meadow of the prince of Duino below Vižovlje. It was a brisk, sunny day. While she was sickling tufts of hay among the rocks by the roadside she heard someone whistling and looked up to see a handsome young fisherman walking toward the road leading down to the sea. "My heart leaped into my mouth," she would later say, and she immediately fell in love.

They were well suited to each other. He was Anton Klarič of Vižovlje, who made his living sometimes by catching fish for sale in Trieste, sometimes by farming, and sometimes as a game warden. Although he stood to inherit his family's house and some land, he was only in part a farmer and was therefore freer than most villagers to fall in love with a woman who could bring him no land or animals as a dowry. For Karlina, he was not only a man who appealed to her in his own right but, one suspects, one who had the advantage of living in a hamlet near the sea and along the railroad. Vižovlje offered just the faintest whiff of the excitement of the city she had come to know as a milkmaid.* The two were married, Karlina moved into the Klaričes' house next door to the Žužeks, and she and Anton produced thirteen children and lived together with a contentment that was proverbial in Vižovlje and the nearby hamlets.

Karlina's case seems to show, on the one hand, that it might be difficult for a surplus young woman to find a satisfactory place for herself in rural society as

---

* It is well known to local people, and often commented on, that young women in the Karst prefer, and have long preferred, to marry men in hamlets nearer to Trieste than their own. Doing so provides a kind of upward social mobility, since such men are less likely to be farmers and more likely to have better-paid jobs linked to the urban economy. Hamlets nearer Trieste are also less isolated, more interesting; from them it may be possible occasionally to visit the city.

a farm wife. It also shows, however, how such a person might be able to enter the marriage market on her own and find a satisfactory husband who was himself the product of changes in the rural economy.

Karlina had in a way defied the old custom of parental matchmaking at just about the same time that Ivan Baptist Žužek was hunting his own bride, and only a decade before Ivan Baptist's nephew, the third Jožef Žužek, quarreled with his widowed mother when he tried to choose his own wife. These breaks, or partial breaks, with the old customs seem to confirm the recollection of old people in the Vižovlje area in the 1970s that it was in about 1900 or 1910 that the custom of parental arrangement of marriages came to an end.[15] Industrialization and urbanization were now offering Karst peasants new ways of making a living outside the traditional farming sector. This change made it both more difficult and less necessary for parents to arrange their children's marriages, particularly when the children were part of the surplus produced by the great decline in mortality, children for whom there simply was not much room in the traditional sector.

The growth of Trieste as a port and industrial center[16] not only stimulated dairying and quarrying in the Karst but also provided jobs in the city for those who wanted them. Slovene blue-collar ghettos developed on the fringe of the city.[17] In these late nineteenth-century decades, none of the younger sons or daughters in the Žužek line we are following went to work in the city, although this was to happen in the next generation. Two of their cousins in Vižovlje, Franc and Ivan Žužek, did take jobs in Trieste, however. What we can learn about their lives there shows how young products of the decline of mortality could indeed find places for themselves in the growing cities. But their stories also suggest what was apparent elsewhere in Europe: that it could be difficult for country people to adjust to urban life.[18]

Franc and Ivan were born in a house in Vižovlje whose back faces No. 2, and they belonged to the branch of the Žužek family known to their neighbors as the "Šteftavi" or "Stevens." Their parents seem to have settled in the hamlet in about 1850 and were almost surely cousins of the line we are following. Their older brother stood to inherit the family house and lands, so Franc and Ivan had to find work elsewhere.

Both brothers found jobs in Trieste during the 1880s, and from police records in the Trieste archives we can catch at least a couple of glimpses of their lives there. Ivan found work making barrels, a common trade in the booming seaport, and when he was about thirty he married a young woman from Mavhinje and had at least one child. The age of marriage is significant. If he had inherited land and become a farmer, he would probably have married at

Fig. 7. Dockside scene in Trieste, about 1890. (*Die österreichisch-ungarische Monarchie [1886–1902 : vol. 10, p. 73].*)

about the age of twenty-five, as many young men in the Karst seem to have done. The fact that he waited until he was thirty suggests that it took him a number of years in the city to achieve even very modest economic security. He and his wife and child lived in a kind of Slovene ghetto on the outskirts of the city. Meanwhile his brother Franc, who was four years younger, slender, and mustachioed, found work as a farrier shoeing horses in a livery stable, a natural job choice for a country boy used to handling animals. He lived near Ivan. According to police records, Franc had had no schooling. The same was probably true of his older brother.

On New Year's Day, 1891, Ivan and Franc, then thirty-three and twenty-nine years old respectively, went to a tavern frequented by Slovene laborers and began drinking. At about 7:00 P.M. they both began to sing. An off-duty policeman in the tavern told them to quiet down, and then the young barmaid came to their table to tell them to pay up and leave. Before she could open her mouth, Franc roared out the first spoken words of a Žužek of which there is any record, to wit: "What do you want, ugly whore?"

The barmaid slapped him, he rose and lurched toward her, a horde of angry patrons of the tavern tried to hold him down, and in the resulting brawl Franc punched the off-duty policeman. Other police were sent for, and the two brothers were led off to jail, with Ivan bellowing that he and his four sons would get even with the police. (In fact, the police record shows, he had only a little daughter.) For his mild resistance to arrest, Ivan spent three days in jail. Franc was tried for having struck the off-duty policeman but was acquitted on the grounds that the policeman had been behind him during the fight and that Franc had hit him without knowing who he was.[19]

Four years later Franc again had dealings with the police, and although he was not the guilty party, the incident tells us something about his life as a villager making his way in the city. He was now thirty-three, had married a Slovene woman, lived in a rented room or rooms, and had been promoted to chief farrier in the livery stable. On his recommendation his boss had fired a farrier named Jožef Mrak, who came from one of the nearby Slovene villages, and hired in his place another young man who had recently finished his military service and who just happened to be Franc's brother-in-law. One day soon thereafter Mrak came to the stable with a gun and fired at Franc, who knocked him down with an iron bar. Franc then retreated into another part of the stable, but he was followed by Mrak, so he hit the man again, this time hurting his hand. The police were called. Mrak was subdued and taken away, and eventually he was sentenced to six months in jail. The police report makes it clear that Franc was the victim, not the guilty party, in this affair, but it also mentions that Franc was "irascible, given to drinking, to excesses, to quarrels." [20]

We must not make too much out of the experiences of these two brothers, but their late marriages, the fact that they lived in a Slovene ghetto, and their humble jobs do suggest that it was hard for country men to make their way in the city. Franc's "drinking" and "excesses" hint at a difficult adjustment to life away from the familiar sounds and smells of Vižovlje and its intimacy and neighborly warmth. [21]

The lives of Ivan Baptist, his cousins Franc and Ivan, and his neighbor Karlina were significantly different from their parents' and ancestors'. In the first place, they were surplus people, products of those little changes in diet and sanitation that, in the second half of the nineteenth century, were permitting children to escape the illnesses that in earlier generations would have slaughtered them. They were lucky to survive, unlucky to be younger children for whom there was no room at home, lucky to live in a time when industries and growing cities offered new livelihoods. They found new ways to live. They arranged their own marriages, resisting or ignoring their parents' wishes. They found new kinds of work. Since they were not farmers, their little home community had little leverage over their behavior. One became mildly eccentric with whimsical pretensions to aristocratic status, even though he was a poor laborer. Two of them left their hamlet to live and work in a city, and there one of them at least may have found the tensions and frustrations of a complex and indifferent society so great that he drank and quarreled. Ivan Baptist, Karlina, Franc, and Ivan were among the first to have to seek new styles of life appropriate to an age of industrialization and human increase.

6

A Peasant in the Machine Age

On the first of May in the year 1910 someone with a camera climbed up the little hill behind Vižovlje to the prehistoric fortification of low stone walls at its summit, turned, pointed his camera down toward the hamlet, and took a photograph of some of the houses and of a locomotive and a couple of railroad cars halted on the tracks on the southwest side of Vižovlje. (See Fig. 8.) The occasion of his taking the picture was the opening of a newly-built, one-room railroad station in the hamlet that was intended to serve bathers from Trieste headed for the shore at the base of the cliffs a mile or so away.

The photograph nicely captures the changes at work on the Karst at the beginning of the twentieth century. In the foreground are a few of Vižovlje's old fieldstone houses and barns (but not, alas, the Žužeks'). Around the hamlet are plowed or spaded fields and rocky, close-cropped pastures, surrounded by the thick walls the peasant serfs of earlier centuries built and added to over generations as they cleared the land of stones. But just beyond the houses is that steam-powered train. The symbol of the Machine Age pauses in the slowly changing hamlet before it charges on across the Karst toward Monfalcone.

This chapter deals with the oldest and the youngest of the sons of Jožef[II], the peasant who had in some ways altered his work life and perhaps his home life as the Karst felt the first ripple effects of industrialization. These two sons continued to work the land, but Jožef[III], the older brother, left Vižovlje for a hamlet farther away from scenes of social and economic change, and there he lived and died a peasant. The younger brother, Valentin, stayed in Vižovlje and worked the family's land. He proved to be, at the same time, both a creature of the old, preindustrial, rural social system and a cautious joiner of the Machine Age. Although his personality was in some ways unique, he illustrates the adaptation many peasants had to make as they moved from one age to the other.

To follow the story of Valentin's adaptation, we must begin at the start of the twentieth century, just after the death of his father, Jožef[II], in 1901. After the oxen had pulled the cart bearing Jožef's dead body back up the dusty road into Vižovlje, six members of the stricken family remained to carry on: Jožef's widow, four sons, and a little daughter. Three other children had died before their father.

Jožef[III]'s survivors would now have to get by without his strength and skill, and get by they would. Half a century earlier, Jožef[I] had taken over the farm work when he was only sixteen, and he had somehow managed. This time there were two young men—Jožef[III], aged twenty-one, and Emil, aged sixteen—fully ready to do the heavier work, and two younger boys, Franc and Valentin, who could help. (See Table 6.) The ratio of hands to mouths was good, and in the short run all would go well.

Fig. 8. A steam locomotive in Vižovlje, 1910. *The dark shape of the train is visible on the tracks beyond the hamlet. In the foreground is most of Vižovlje, but the Žužeks' house is just to the left of the area shown. Around the hamlet are the rocky fields and pastures, dotted with stunted trees, with which generations of Žužeks had to contend.*

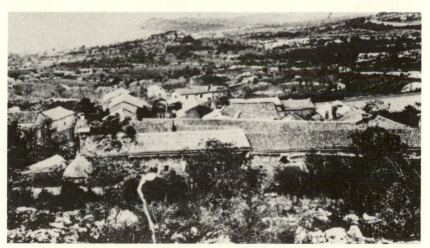

TABLE 6
Children of Jožef" (1853–1901) and Marija (1852–1928), with Recorded Causes of Death

	DATES	RECORDED OR KNOWN CAUSE OF DEATH
Jožef^{III}	1880–?	[adult]
Ivan	1882–98	tuberculosis
Emil	1885–1956	pneumonia?
Franc	1888–1978	stroke
Alojzij	1890–90 (14 days)	"weakness"
Valentin	1891–1979	arteriosclerosis
Hubert	1893–95	dysentery
Marija	1896–1935	tuberculosis

But what about the longer run? The family's real problem was a population surplus; the Žužeks had several of what, in the previous chapter, we called surplus people. They could not all stay in the house, marry, and raise families there, and survive on the thirteen small parcels of rocky land left by their father.[1] There simply was not enough room for all.

Who, then, would inherit the house and land? Would everything go to the oldest son, Jožef^{III}, or would the inheritance be divided in equal shares among the children? The answer could profoundly affect their lives. Not surprisingly, in view of his early death, Jožef^{II} had left no will, but presumably his wife and children knew well enough that he had intended that the house and land should go to Jožef^{III}. In fact, there is some evidence that this was his plan. Several years before his death Jožef^{II} had apprenticed his second oldest son, Ivan, to a shoemaker in nearby Mavhinje.[2] Ivan had died soon afterward of tuberculosis, but the fact that his father had made this arrangement for his second son suggests that he had expected to leave his house and land to the oldest.

And of course the heads of the Žužek family had always left their property to their oldest sons. In former times, indeed, the lords of Duino had required each serf family to pass their property on intact to one son because it was in their interest to have peasants with enough land to permit them to pay their dues and to maintain oxen and carts to use for their labor services. In 1901, however, the Duino lords naturally had no say in what their former subjects did with the land that they now owned themselves. It is also true that a wind

of egalitarianism had long been blowing across Europe and that in many lands
families of all classes were now obliged by law to leave considerable parts of
their estates to all of their children.[3] But it still suited Karst farmers to use the
system of primogeniture. In this way, they no doubt still reasoned, their oldest
sons and their families at least would have enough to live on.

In any case, almost everything went to Jožef[III]. The younger Žužek brothers and their sister made no complaints as their older brother took over the
house, the small barn, and the furnishings, tools, fields, pastures, and woodlots.[4] Perhaps they accepted the harsh, Malthusian reasonableness of primogeniture, or perhaps they were more or less satisfied with the small portions
that they eventually received. When custom bestowed the lion's share on the
oldest brother, it also demanded that he give something, at least, to his
younger brothers and perhaps very small dowries to his sisters. After a decade
had passed and Jožef[III] had been able to save some money, he gave Emil,
Franc, and Valentin one hundred florins apiece. Years later, as an old man,
Franc would say, not bitterly but as if it were a matter of fact, that a hundred
florins was "nothing." In fact each of these three portions may have equaled
about a tenth of Jožef's inheritance.[5] As for his little sister, Marija, however,
her share was indeed nothing.

The portions that the younger Žužek brothers received show that the old
rural family system, by this time in its last days, was not always quite as harsh
as one might suppose. In some places, indeed, primogeniture did give everything to the oldest son and throw the others off the land and into poverty.[6]
But on the Karst, even though there was so little to go around, the harshness
of the inheritance system was mitigated a little by portions for the younger
sons and sometimes by small dowries for the daughters. In fact, we have already seen that younger sons in the Žužek family did not invariably wander off
from the village and die by the roadside. One brother of Jožef[II] had married and
moved to Mavhinje to farm; as far as we can see, he lived there about as well as
his older brother did in Vižovlje.[7] Another brother, Ivan Baptist, had become a
quarryman, bought a little house in Vižovlje, and somehow scraped by.

Suppose, however, that a younger son wanted not merely to remain in his
village but also to take over the house and land of his older brother. Was such
a violation of stern custom possible? Just such a question would arise in the
Žužek household early in the twentieth century. After Jožef[III] had inherited
the house and land, his wiry, sharp-tongued mother, his ten-year-old brother
Valentin, and his little sister Marija remained in the house with him. The two
teen-aged brothers, Emil and Franc, fairly soon left the house and became
laborers, and we shall have much more to say about them in the next chapter

because they illustrate very well the ways in which younger sons could try to adapt to the process of industrialization. But here we will follow what happened to Jožef[III] and Valentin, the two brothers who stayed on the land.[8]

No two brothers could have been less alike. Jožef[III] was a mild and docile young man whose mother contemptuously called him "Aunty." Valentin, by contrast, was harsh and grasping. A photograph he posed for during his Austro-Hungarian army training (Fig. 9) strongly suggests his toughness and self-confidence. Somehow he became his mother's favorite, perhaps because she admired his will to survive and prosper.

With his hundred florins and perhaps other savings as well, Valentin bought a team of horses and a cart and found work hauling stone from a quarry in Nabrežina, just as his father had done on a part-time basis. Taking advantage of Jožef's good nature, he pastured his horses in his brother's fields, sheltered them in his brother's shed, and paid nothing for his own food and shelter in his brother's house. He prospered as a carter, especially perhaps during World War I, when he was exempted from military service and stayed home. (He had been born lacking the tips to two fingers on his right hand and thus could not fire a rifle.) After a decade had passed, he had saved a considerable sum.

Meanwhile his mother made life unpleasant for Jožef[III] and found reason to object when he wished to marry a local young woman. Jožef submitted in everything to his mother and brother, but finally, when he was forty-two, he met and decided to marry a young woman from the inland village of Brje who had no brothers or sisters and therefore stood to inherit her parents' property. He sold everything to Valentin for a small sum, married his peasant heiress, and left Vižovlje for good. (Years later, his brother Franc's daughter Berta visited Brje when she was about twelve, helping her aunt and uncle with their farm work. She recalls her uncle Jožef as a mild and henpecked old man [actually he must have been fifty-five] who was much concerned about drying some of his grapes so that he would have something sweet to nibble on during the winter.)

Valentin, who had begun life with the economic handicap of being a younger son, had broken the chain of inheritance by the oldest son and was now the owner of the Žužek house and land. Like Jacob in the book of Genesis, with his mother's support he had taken over his brother's birthright and supplanted him as owner of the Žužeks' house and land.[9] The lesson seems to be that even a custom so essential to the harsh realities of the Karst as primogeniture could be violated by a man of energy and strong will.

Fig. 9. Valentin Žužek (1891–1979), while in military service, about 1912.

Now we must see how Valentin continued, and perhaps completed, the
transition from peasant to farmer and citizen that his grandfather and father
had begun. To do this, we must first pose a problem of definition.

What is a peasant? There is no easy answer. Peasant societies of the past and present are so numerous and so infinitely varied that a satisfactory, comprehensive definition is impossible. Let us therefore merely say that typical European peasants at the beginning of the nineteenth century usually had these qualities:

1. They farmed chiefly in order to feed themselves and the landowners, and were more subsistence than market farmers.
2. They were viewed by most others as socially inferior.
3. They had little or no political power, except for the threat of revolt.
4. They were illiterate, and partly as a result of this they were ignorant of the world beyond their horizons.

For several generations before Valentin was a young man, the Žužeks had been slowly shedding some of these peasant characteristics. As far as the first part of our description is concerned, probably even Tomaž and Matija had produced partly for the market. Almost surely they sold a little of their wool to traveling buyers for textile mills and, occasionally, a superannuated ox to a butcher. Even Valentin's grandfather and father, however, do not seem to have moved very far toward market farming. Instead, when Jožef[I] and Jožef[II] wanted to expand their incomes they had become part-time haulers of water and stone.

In 1848 the Žužeks ceased to belong to a class of former serfs still legally considered to be their landlords' subjects. There is no doubt that after that date their betters still considered them to be dirty yokels, and Slovene ones at that, but they were not quite so inferior as before. A little later the men acquired the right to vote. Their votes counted for less than those of bigger taxpayers, but they had gained some measure of political power.

With respect to the first three parts of our description, then, the Žužeks at the end of the nineteenth century were no longer completely peasants. They were in transition. As for the last criterion, their awareness and understanding of the outside world was probably not very different from what it had been at the beginning of the century. Perhaps the right to vote had in some ways enlarged their outlook, and their stone hauling may have brought them into contact with a wider range of people and ideas, but they were still unschooled and illiterate.

In two specific ways, Valentin would cease to be what we have called a typical peasant. Let us consider literacy first. What kind of education did he receive?

Part of his education had been the traditional one of peasant children. As a little boy he, like his brothers and sisters, had of course done a great deal of farm work, first helping with small chores and then with bigger ones. As he did these chores, his parents were his teachers. From Jožef[II] and Marija he learned first such things as how to sickle hay and take cows to pasture and later how to yoke and lead oxen and how to make decisions about what to plant. At the same time he probably learned some of his parents' values and attitudes: an oxlike acceptance of hard work, humility toward his betters, unreflective piety, and stoic resignation to the deaths of others around him. Like peasant children elsewhere, he learned much of what he needed to know by serving a kind of occupational apprenticeship with his parents.[10]

Valentin, however, had also been going through a form of preparation for life that Jožef[II] and Marija had never known. During the nineteenth century, the Austro-Hungarian government, recognizing that it needed better-educated soldiers and workers, had founded a great many elementary and secondary schools and had begun to require its people to attend them up to the age of fourteen. This modernizing drive was slow to reach the Karst, and in the early 1860s most peasants in the Vižovlje area could only sign the emancipation agreements ending their payments to Duino by clumsily scrawling X's after their names. Beginning in 1854 there was a one-room school in Mavhinje that functioned six months a year.[11] Attendance did not become compulsory, however, until about 1890.[12]

Jožef[III], oldest of the children, was born too early to be subject to the new requirement, and he never learned to read and write, although he is said to have been able to do sums quickly on his fingers. Ivan (who died at sixteen of tuberculosis), Emil, Franc, Valentin, and Marija, however, all went to school. Each day until they were fourteen the five children trudged up the rough road to Mavhinje, where the schoolmaster gave them and about eighty others a grounding in reading, writing, and arithmetic. These five Žužek children seem to have absorbed a solid elementary-school education.[13]

Valentin had, then, at least acquired a tool—literacy—with which to strip off the insularity of the peasant and comprehend the world beyond the Karst. Whether he in fact did acquire some of this larger understanding is hard to say. As we shall see, he was a man who worked almost constantly, ignoring virtually everything but his cattle and his land. On Sunday mornings after church his brother Franc, a product of the same amount of formal education, used to sit in his kitchen next door and read his weekly newspaper. Valentin was likely to be heading out to his fields.

The mention of Valentin's work in the fields brings us to the other way in which he almost completely ceased to be a peasant. One thing that was characteristic of European peasants in the early nineteenth century, we said, was that they farmed chiefly to feed themselves. Valentin's great-great-grandfather and his great-grandfather did that, although they may have used some of what they produced to pay rent to their former lords at the castle of Duino. His grandfather and father also were largely subsistence farmers—and in that respect, therefore, peasants—although they did haul water and stone to earn some money.

Unlike his grandfather and father, Valentin concentrated solely on farming, and unlike any of his ancestors, so far as one can tell, he farmed energetically for the market. He had, indeed, done some stone hauling as a young man, but after he took over his brother's land he apparently decided to concentrate on farming. Perhaps, as a younger son who had taken the place of the oldest, he particularly relished the traditional farming role and wished to enjoy it unsullied by any other kind of work. Perhaps, like many South Slavs of his time, he viewed farming as superior to industrial work.[14] And perhaps he realized that with the continued growth of Trieste and other markets a farmer could now make an adequate living without having to do other part-time work. In any case, for the rest of his working life Valentin not only grew food for his family and himself but also seems to have produced far more for the market than the earlier Žužeks had. He increased his herd of cattle until he had not only the usual two oxen and a cow but about four additional cows, a considerable number for the Karst in the first half of the twentieth century. He became perhaps half subsistence farmer and half dairy and truck-farming specialist, sending milk and vegetables to market in Trieste each day.

With both his literacy and his market farming, then, Valentin ceased to be a peasant. It is not easy to say just what we should call him—a citizen farmer, perhaps?—but he clearly belonged to a social category different from that of his ancestors.

Valentin not only concentrated on farming; he also adjusted the way he farmed to changing conditions. He did not aggressively, knowingly take part in an agricultural revolution like the one that had already transformed the agriculture of western Europe and was now changing that of the less progressive center and east.[15] He did, however, make the myriad adjustments, big and little, that Karst farmers had to make in their use of the land if they wanted to profit from the steady growth of Trieste and Monfalcone and the villages immediately around them.

All over Europe farmers were substituting new strains of cattle, the products of breeding skill and genetic science in the more advanced countries, for the local races their ancestors had raised for centuries. When Valentin had occasion to buy cattle to replace those he had bought from Jožef[III], he bought the hardy Swiss type that was then being introduced into the Karst. The light-brown Swiss cows produced more milk than the local breed, and the oxen, the castrated males, could pull a plow or a cart harder and for a longer time. Moreover, their hooves were tough enough to cope with the rocks in his pastures. When Valentin bought a pig, he purchased one of the newly introduced white Yorkshires, prolific beasts with much lean meat on their bones.[16]

Valentin may also have learned by word of mouth of new ways of caring for his livestock. At the end of World War I, a young farmer named Ivan Legiša from the nearby hamlet of Medja vas came home with astounding reports about advanced methods of stock raising that he had observed in France. These apparently created a local sensation.[17] Perhaps Valentin, who must have known Legiša, learned of these new methods and began to use them.

During his working lifetime, the services and resources for a farmer in Vižovlje improved fairly steadily. As we have said, even before Valentin took over the Žužek land, a small railroad station was built in Vižovlje. Now at least some of the trains that had formerly whistled past the hamlet stopped there to drop off and pick up Triestines on their way to and from the seashore a mile or so away, as well as farm people from the Vižovlje area. As a result, Valentin could easily send his milk and vegetables (his cash crops) to Trieste with a neighbor's wife. He could also go by train a few miles to the northwest and buy tools and seeds at the farm supply stores in the growing town of Monfalcone. After World War I, the Italian government, which had just taken over the area, laid a pipe across the Karst and brought water to public faucets just below the hamlet. Now Valentin no longer had to take his cattle to drink at the man-made, rain-filled pond in the village common, nor, when that went dry, did he have to cart water in barrels from the Timavo River. The local roads were also improved, and after World War II Vižovlje had electricity. In short, then, Valentin benefited as a farmer from a succession of services that made it easier for him to produce food and get it to market.

But Valentin was no agricultural innovator. He was simply a typical small farmer in a place that was slowly benefiting from the growth of an urban market and from some of the farm technology of western Europe. He seems to have accepted those changes that would clearly benefit him and ignored the others. For instance, he refused for years to buy a tractor. Why should he throw away his money, he asked, when it was easy enough to raise and use oxen as his ancestors had done? (He finally gave in on this matter in the late 1950s when his youngest son Bruno took over most of the farm work and persuaded him to make the purchase.)

Only after he had taken over the family house and land in about 1920, and only after he had begun to change to a market-directed style of farming, did Valentin decide to marry and raise a family. Any Karst farmer needed help with his work, but knowing Valentin's determination to make the most of what he had and his penuriousness (which we will discuss below), we can be sure that economic considerations pushed him into marriage. He was now thirty-five, and he had no one to help him in the fields and no one to do much of the housework and the lighter farm chores. His mother was seventy-four, and in only two years she would die of what the priest would list as "the wasting away of old age." His sister Marija was also wasting away, but with tuberculosis. She was useless to him, merely a mouth to feed, and in his frustration he beat her from time to time.

Valentin therefore no doubt calculated that he needed a wife to help him and to bear sons to work in the fields. (He may also have wanted a son to inherit the house and lands that he had managed with such effort to take over from Jožef[III].) In 1926 he married a farmer's daughter, Justina Lupinc (*lu peents'*) from the remote hamlet of Praprot. (A century earlier, as we noted, his great-grandfather Matija had also married a Lupinc from the same tiny place.) Justina moved into house No. 2, helped her husband with the farm work, and in short order produced two children. When she was in childbed the third time, however, she could not give birth, and the midwife told Valentin to take his wife to the hospital in Monfalcone for a Caesarean section. They set off in a borrowed horse cart, but Justina and her unborn baby died en route. Within a year, in 1932, Valentin married again. In a hamlet even more remote than Praprot he found his second wife, a plain, stocky woman who wore her kerchief far down over her forehead.

According to most of those who knew him, Valentin was always a hard-driving, hard-bitten man, and he was especially so to his children. To them he had little to say but "Work! Get to work!" He was especially hard with his children by his first wife, Stanko and Milka, and in this he was abetted by his second wife, Marija, who stepped easily into the role of harsh stepmother. She was especially unpleasant to the children after Milka wandered behind the house one day and found her stepmother in a compromising attitude with a young man.

To complete our picture of the ways in which Valentin strove to prosper, we must include some mention of his penuriousness. Unlike most of the people of Vižovlje, he would give nothing to beggars who knocked at the door

Fig. 10. Valentin Žužek and family, 1946. *The cart carries leaves to be used as litter in cattle stalls.*

and asked for food. (When he shouted "Nothing!" to one hungry woman who came to his kitchen door one day, she pointed to his children at the table and screamed, "One day one of these children will be a beggar!" As yet this has not happened.) His family ate only what they produced on their land, and they wore their clothes until they barely held together. Valentin himself was especially scruffy. To save razor blades and soap, and time for work, he shaved only occasionally and usually had several days' growth of whiskers. The people of Vižovlje, with their Slavic love of nicknames, dubbed him "Hedgehog." * On one occasion he reported with some satisfaction, after returning from Monfalcone, that as he had entered a store there the owner had taken him for a beggar and handed him a coin.

Valentin was, then, a very hard worker and a very thrifty head of household. Were these the qualities of the peasant he was ceasing to be, or of the market farmer he was becoming? Not the former, if the anthropologist George Foster is correct. "In the traditional peasant society," he writes, "hard work and thrift are moral qualities of only the slightest functional value." If land is scarce and technology is primitive, hard work does not pay off, and if people live in a subsistence economy, they are already "at the margin," and there is nothing to be thrifty about.[18] In the Karst, however, as I pointed out in Chapter 2, it appears that peasants did in fact work hard, and I suspect that they were also thrifty. But of course, hard work and penny-pinching can also be useful for a market farmer. In Valentin's case, these qualities of his were probably the results not only of his peasant upbringing but also of his needs as a market farmer and especially of his own nature.

Valentin was also very suspicious of and hostile to those around him. Let one example suffice. On a Saturday morning in June 1938 he climbed the slope behind his house to the edge of his property and began to pick the cherries from one of his trees, dropping them over his left shoulder into an old wicker rucksack strapped to his back. At noon he took off the rucksack, left it on the ground under the tree, and went to his house for lunch. When he returned he found the basket broken and the cherries gone. In a rage he ran down the hill and into the house of his brother Franc, who lived next door. For years the two brothers had been on somewhat distant terms. Franc and his family were eating lunch. "Franc," Valentin shouted, adding a few expletives, "I know what you did. You broke my basket and stole my cherries." The accusation was foolish; Franc had a cherry tree of his own, enjoyed a reputation for honesty, and was no prankster.[19] He angrily denied the charge. "You dirty liar," Valentin yelled, and he stormed out of the house. For the rest of their lives, until Franc died four decades later, the two brothers, living in adjoining houses, never spoke to each other again.

Foster believes that this kind of suspiciousness and even hostility toward those around one is, contrary to a widespread opinion, quite typical of peasants. In his view, peasants often distrust and criticize their neighbors, who are competitors in a harsh struggle for existence, in order to keep the neighbors

---

* A friendly and outgoing farmer in Mavhinje was known as "Good day!" A Sicilian who came to Sistiana after World War II and peddled sardines, squid, and sea bass in the nearby hamlets was called "Fish." Halpern (1967: 164) tells of a Serbian woman with a wide mouth and toothy grin who was known in her village as "Crocodile."

from taking advantage of them.[20] Valentin's behavior may not have been typical of the way peasants behaved in Vižovlje, however. In the recollections of old people of the hamlet, before World War II or thereabout the people of Vižovlje were generally "united" and got along well together.[21] Here again, Valentin seems to have been unique unto himself.

Did Valentin, the younger son who had taken over his brother's inheritance, also make himself a rich man? Hardly. For a farmer on the Karst that goal was out of reach. Valentin and his family no doubt lived better than the nineteenth-century Žužeks, but they worked very hard,[22] dressed poorly, and ate very simply.

It seems likely that Valentin's drive, his stinginess, his terribly hard labor, and his forcing his children to work were directed chiefly at keeping what he had. He was a supplanter. He had taken over the house and land of an older brother, the inheritor, and he wanted to make absolutely sure that he never lost what he had won.

Obscure villager though he was, Valentin managed to make quite a remarkable transition during the first half of his life. First, simply by going obediently to school as a boy and learning to read and write, he had shed the

Fig. 11. Women and children of Mavhinje, after church, early in World War I. *In the left rear is a soldier, the only man in the group, who was probably home on leave. Note the bare feet and the girl with a toothache whose jaw is wrapped with a handkerchief, second row on the right. In the right rear is the house of the earlier Franc Žužek, son of Jožef[1]; soon after this photograph was taken an artillery shell struck the house and killed Franc's wife, Jožefa.*

illiteracy that had been a part of his family's peasant past. Then, using his quarry earnings, he had broken with ancient custom by buying the family's house and land from his oldest brother. In this way he had forced his way into a very traditional role, that of the peasant farmer who grows food mainly for his own subsistence. Having done this, however, he had then picked up the skills and outlook of a farmer growing food mainly for the market. It may not have been what he had set out to do, but Valentin ended by leaving the world of the peasant for that of the small farmer in the Machine Age.

7

Slots for Proletarians

While Valentin was shaping his own destiny and that of Jožef^{III}, and tuberculosis was doing the same for Marija, their brothers Franc and Emil set out to seek their fortunes.

These two were products of the widespread decline in deaths from disease and undernourishment that, together with higher birthrates, was making populations swiftly rise. Earlier, that rise had produced a trickle of migrants from the land. Their uncle Ivan Baptist and their cousins Ivan and Emil had been part of that movement of surplus people. But now the trickle had become a flood, and Emil and Franc belonged to that horde of young men and women who were leaving work on the land and trying to find slots for themselves in the booming economy of the industrializing Western world.[1]

There is a moment in the process of industrialization almost anywhere when country people are torn between two worlds. On one horizon are the fields and woods that they have always known. On the other are the mills and the building scaffolds of the rising towns a few miles away where they may be able to find jobs that, however humble, pay better than the old agriculture.

During this early stage in the industrialization process, country people often find their places on a continuum between the two worlds. Some, like Jožef^I and Jožef^{II} stay on the land but supplement their incomes with part-time jobs connected with new industries. Some of the men stay on the land but work in the towns on weekdays and on the farm on weekends, while their wives take over much of the daily routine of farm work. Some men and women, especially those without land of their own, move back and forth between the country and the town, according to the season and the state of the business cycle, now tending bobbins or shoveling coal, now helping farmers back in their villages to bring in their hay.[2] But many others pour into the towns and stay there. In the early twentieth century the women who did this scrubbed floors, tended power looms, served beer, sold fruit, and, sometimes, sold themselves. The men oiled motors, stoked boilers, paved roads, shoveled snow, groomed horses, heaved barrels, and, sometimes, begged and stole. When the greatest war in history broke out in 1914, these proletarians did much of the fighting.

Where on this continuum between the village and the city would Emil and Franc find places for themselves? How would they fare? What mental adjustments would they have to make?

Both Emil and Franc were short and slender, like their mother and their brothers and sister. Emil was blond; Franc, dark. Emil was sometimes pleasant, sometimes harsh and sullen, while Franc was quiet, humorous, engaging. When separately they set out from home, both already knew some things that would help them to earn their livings away from the farm. Both were used to hard physical work and knew how to use a pick and shovel and how to deal with draft animals. They could read and write and do sums, though perhaps they would never make much use of these skills.[3] And they had learned both at home and at school how to take orders.

Emil's story, I suggest, is that of a man who could not adjust to the life of a landless laborer in exile from his native hamlet. Once he had left his home and the stability of peasant life, he lacked the strength of character to shape a satisfying life for himself in the new industrial society.

Since he had inherited no land and was not a favorite of his mother's like Valentin, Emil had to leave home in his mid-teens. He set off on his travels, which never really stopped until his death.[4] He was something like the protagonist of a well-known Slovene novel, Ivan Cankar's *The Bailiff Yerney and His Rights*. Looking back on his youth when he was an old man, Jernej says to an acquaintance, "Where did I come from? From Resje, I believe; yes, from Resje I came. There were too many of us at home, so I had to go. It is so long ago that I never think of my mother or my brothers, and were they to pass me on the road, I should not know them."[5]

Equipped with only a rudimentary education, stigmatized as a man of the under class by his Slovene name and looks, handicapped by a love of the bottle, what could Emil do? He became an itinerant laborer, wandering from place to place and taking what work he could find. For a while he served as apprentice to a tailor in a town on the Dalmatian coast of what is now Yugoslavia. According to one who knew him there, he was rarely to be seen without a bottle in his hand. At some point he did his Austrian military service, and later he fought in World War I and was wounded badly enough to need hospitalization in Vienna. After the war he was back on his travels again. Eventually he made his way to Trieste. The younger children of the country people often finally settled there, just as the shells of crustaceans had settled on the Karst when it was the bottom of the sea.

Living on the edge of the city, Emil barely managed to survive by buying and selling horses, a business natural enough for one who had grown up on the Karst. One day, however, he bought a stolen horse (unknowingly, it is said) and then sold it. The owner found the horse and reported the matter to the police, and Emil went to jail. After his release he found a job as night watchman in a warehouse in the port area of Trieste, and at about the same time he married. He appeared for the moment to be settling into a more or less stable place among the city's largely Slovene proletariat.

Emil's wife was the product of circumstances much harder than his own. She had been abandoned as a baby on the doorstep of a shopkeeper in Ljubljana, about eighty miles by rail from Trieste. Ljubljana was then a town of some forty thousand with a hinterland of pretty hills and valleys dotted with tiny Slovene villages. We can feel fairly sure that Olga's mother was unmarried. Until well into the twentieth century, an unmarried and pregnant Slovene farm girl was usually very harshly treated. Her family, terribly ashamed of her pregnancy and aware that they could never find her a husband, were likely to beat her and drive her from home. She would then wander from village to village, an outcast, or try to lose herself in a town. There were no homes for unmarried mothers and no adoption agencies. When she gave birth, no one would take the child off her hands, and she could not both work and take care of the child.[6] In several stories written by Cankar early in the twentieth century, an unwed mother is forced to abandon her baby, or she is persecuted and dies, leaving her child to suffer poverty and cruelty.[7]

Olga was probably the child of such an unmarried mother who had been forced to abandon her baby girl. Generously enough, the shopkeeper and his wife raised her with their children to the age of fourteen. Then they told her that it would be unfair to their own children if they had to spend more of their limited income on her and that she must now fend for herself. Olga, therefore, like her future husband, somehow made her way to Trieste. There she found work as a housemaid. She also became the mistress of a Triestine and had two illegitimate daughters by him. Eventually she met Emil Žužek, another rootless being, and when he asked her to marry him, she did.

While he was on duty as night watchman one night, Emil broke open a case of liquor in the warehouse. The next morning his employer found him dead drunk and fired him. Emil's wife persuaded the man to rehire her husband, but presently Emil again drank on the job, and this time he was fired for good. So now he made his way back to his home on the Karst. For a while he and his wife, two stepdaughters, and baby son lived in a decrepit house that he rented in Sistiana, a mile or so from Vižovlje. Emil found work in the stone quarries of Nabrežina, but he continued to drink, and when he drank he beat his wife and the children. Finally they left him. Not long afterward Emil was fired from the quarrying job, and again he took up his life as an itinerant worker. Sometimes he was to be found as far away as Milan, in north central Italy, and sometimes he turned up in and around Vižovlje and Sistiana. When he did, his brother Franc's wife, Lojza, would urge him to stop drinking and return to his family.

Years passed, and Emil lost all touch with his family. Olga found work as a domestic servant again in Trieste and managed somehow to raise her three children. Her son, her only child by Emil, finished his schooling and became a truck driver. On one occasion, while passing through Sistiana, he decided to look up his father, whom he had not seen since he was a child. He stopped his truck and walked up to a group of men resting at noonday from their work repairing the road. "Do any of you know a man around here named Emil Žužek?" he asked. One of them, quite old and perhaps none too sober, rose to his feet. "I'm Emil Žužek," he said. "Who wants to know?"

Some years later Olga lay dying in a hospital in Trieste. When her daughter Roberta came to visit her, a doctor remarked to her that there was another patient with the same last name as her mother's who was dying of pneumonia in one of the men's wards. Roberta went to see him. The man was Emil. "Who are you?" he asked. When she told him that she was his stepdaughter, he murmured "Ah, darling!" It was the first time that he had ever used any term of endearment to her. He died soon after.

While Emil was lurching through his futile life as a perennially displaced farm boy, his younger brother Franc started out on a similar course but with happier results.[8] Franc, one might say, almost completed the transition from farming to industry that his grandfather had tentatively begun when he first used his ox cart to haul water to the workmen carving a railroad through the Karst. In making the transition he seems to have been helped by a strength of character that was lacking in Emil, and also by a wise decision about where to live.

When he was about thirteen, Franc was considered old enough to take over occasionally his father's job of hauling blocks of marble from the Nabrežina quarries to the stonecutters in Friuli. His reward for this task came when, having delivered the stone, he bought himself some rolls from a baker who lived near the stonecutters. Eating these plain white rolls on the easy return trip was heaven itself.

Franc also, as was mentioned earlier, received some formal education. After he had finished his schooling at the age of fourteen, he worked for only a couple of years on the Žužek lands. As with Emil, there was no place for him at home. In any case, Franc did not agree with his brother Valentin and many other Slovenes, for whom farming was worthier and socially superior to other manual labor.[9] To him farming was grim and dirty work. Although he loved his hamlet and all his life he raised chickens and tended a large garden, he was happy to escape the grinding toil that had filled the lives of his ancestors.

At the age of sixteen Franc left home for his first job, and for the next half century he held so many jobs that he could not, at the end of his working life, remember them all. We will consider only some of those that he held in his first decade of work, to give an impression of the character of the work he did and the ease and almost indifference with which he moved from one job to the next. He began in 1904, when he and a cousin found work digging holes for telegraph poles in the Istrian Peninsula south of Trieste. Soon he returned home and worked for a few years in a quarry at Nabrežina. He may have held another job or two, and at some point he had a year of compulsory military training in the Austro-Hungarian army at a camp in Istria. Then in 1911 an English-owned firm opened a shipyard in Monfalcone on the coast to the west of Vižovlje. Here Franc found a job in a supply yard, helping to store the huge timbers used in naval construction. Later he drove a horse-drawn wagon and hauled the timbers from the railroad freight cars to the shipyard. Presently he left the shipyard and went back to Nabrežina to work for a little company that hauled broken stone from the quarries down a steep road to the coast of the Adriatic Sea, where the stone was loaded onto boats to be carried to builders in Trieste.

As he worked, Franc adapted to new ways. One day, when he was eighteen, he was walking to his job in one of the quarries in Nabrežina. A bicycle salesman approached him and suggested that he could save time if he would buy a bicycle and ride to work. The price was 120 florins. "How could I ever pay?" Franc asked. The salesman then explained to him the mysteries of monthly payments, presumably including interest. So Franc bought a new but rudimentary bicycle, and he practiced riding it on the old Roman road until he could cope with its greatest defect, a lack of brakes. He could now move along the Karst roads much faster than any of his ancestors had ever done. Later, when he worked in the shipyard in Monfalcone, he tried to make another adaptation to modern life, but with less success. While working there he came to admire the dashing appearance of the company's pipe-smoking, young English engineers. For Franc, their pipes somehow symbolized their modernity and sophistication. Finally he bought himself a pipe and some tobacco and tried out this engaging custom. The results were so violent and unpleasant that he never smoked again.

Franc was now a young man in his twenties. He was short and wiry, well made for swinging a pick or hefting a boulder onto a wagon. He had dark and curly hair, a deeply tanned face, and a tiny moustache hiding under his nose.

A short time before the outbreak of World War I, Franc bought a house after becoming engaged to a local young woman (the engagement was eventually broken off). The purchase reveals much about the way he handled his money and the way he saw his future. He bought a house not in Nabrežina, Monfalcone, Trieste, or some other place where he was likely to work, but in Vižovlje. In fact, the house shared its southeast wall with the old Žužek house, No. 2, in which he had grown up. The old couple who had owned Franc's house (not surprisingly, they were Gabrovices) had been typical small-scale farmers, although Franc bought no fields or woodlands with the house. On the southeast side of the ground floor was a room with stalls for two or three animals, and on the northwest side was an all-purpose eating and living room with a typical Karst chimney kitchen projecting into the courtyard. Upstairs were a bedroom and a hayloft, and above them was a low-ceilinged attic for sleeping or for storing grain and potatoes. Behind the house there was room for a large vegetable garden. The house cost "very little," according to Franc, and he paid for it with his inheritance portion and what he had saved from his earnings in the last decade. Later he converted the stalls and hayloft into bedrooms, and eventually he added a stone-walled privy and a chicken house.

The purchase of the house and the alterations he made in it show clearly that Franc had decided to remain in his hamlet. He would be a laborer who lived in a village. He would not farm like Valentin, but neither would he move to the city or wander from one place of work to another like Emil. He had no desire to be rescued by industrialization from what Marx and Engels once called "the idiocy of rural life."[10]

Franc was in Monfalcone on July 28, 1914, when Austria declared war on Serbia and a general European war became likely. He heard a priest tell the sad news to a crowd of workmen in the main square of the little industrial town. Many of the men wept as they foresaw the misery to come. Indeed, Italy and Austria would do much of their bloodiest fighting in the area stretching from the northern Karst to the Alpine foothills around Caporetto. Much of the action would be in the northern end of what had once been the fief of the lords of Duino. The horrors of war would be especially hard on poor farmers and laborers and their families who had almost none of the chauvinism and national greed that had brought about this cataclysm.

Vižovlje, Mavhinje, and Cerovlje lay just on the Austrian side of the strategically important Mount Ermada (directly north of Duino), so these hamlets suffered heavily during the war. From rafts on the Adriatic, Italian guns lobbed shells onto the Karst. The shelling nearly flattened Vižovlje and badly damaged the nearby hamlets.[11] A shell fragment killed Franc's aunt as she prepared food at her kitchen table in her house in Mavhinje (see Fig. 12). Most of the people of these hamlets fled inland and spent periods of the war crowded into cattle sheds in distant hamlets. In 1915, hunger, dysentery, and typhus raised the annual toll of deaths in the three hamlets from the normal eighteen or so to forty.[12]

Franc, like his brothers Jožef[III] and Emil, was drafted immediately,[13] and for several years he took part in some of the hardest fighting of the war. Battles usually began with the Austro-Hungarian soldiers shouting "Hurrah!" and the Italians shouting "Italia!" or various regimental cries. The shouting was followed by rifle and machine-gun fire and the throwing of grenades, with Franc doing his share of both. The battles often culminated in toe-to-toe bayonet fighting, sometimes at night, with soldiers lunging in a kind of drunken frenzy at enemies they could barely make out in the darkness. In one such battle Franc was wounded, and he spent several months recovering in a hospital in Vienna.

The periods of fighting alternated with periods of rest, recuperation, and delousing, and during one of these intervals Franc and a friend had a taste of army discipline. In an abandoned village the two young men had dug up some spring potatoes, and they began to cook them over a fire in the woods near Lake Doberdob, some miles northwest of Duino. An Austrian officer rode by, saw the fire, and had the two arrested because the smoke might have caught the enemy's attention. He ordered them tied to a tree in such a way that their toes could barely touch the ground—a painful position. After the officer had left, a sergeant loosened their bonds enough so that they could get their feet on the ground, and after a few hours they were released.

Like the other farm boys and laborers beside him, Franc had almost no idea what he was supposed to be fighting for. He did feel some loyalty to Francis Joseph. He had been named for the emperor (his full name was Franc

Jožef), and he had been taught to revere him. Years before, his teacher had taken Franc and his schoolmates to the train station in Nabrežina so that they could see their ruler as he passed through on his way to Trieste. Franc would always remember Francis Joseph affectionately as an old man with side whiskers who waved to the children as his train rolled through the station. But what loyalty could Franc have felt to the huge and polyglot empire Francis Joseph ruled? Or to the harsh and alien officers, most of whom came from elsewhere in central Europe? Or to his fellow soldiers from deeper in the Bal-

Fig. 12. Marija Žužek (1896–1935).

kan Peninsula, who horrified him with their bloodthirstiness? They were more foreign to him than the Italian army. Why then did he fight? Because he was told to.

When the tide of war turned in favor of Italy and her allies in 1918, Franc was captured and sent to Genoa as a prisoner. He was assigned to a hospital, and because he came from a border area he was able to serve as an interpreter, translating for the Italian doctors the words of wounded Austrian prisoners. At the end of 1918 the war ended, and Franc and thousands of other prisoners went home.

When Franc—barefoot, dirty, and hungry—arrived back in Vižovlje at the end of the war, he found his hamlet nearly leveled. Italian cannons had reduced his own recently purchased house, the old family home (No. 2) next door, and most of the others almost to a rubble of the Karstian fieldstones from which, centuries earlier, they had been built.

Something else much larger had also collapsed. The defeated Hapsburg empire had been dissolved. Trieste and its hinterland in the Karst as far east as the widely known limestone caves at Postojna were lopped off the carcass of the old supranational state and handed over to victorious Italy. The Žužeks were now Italians.

In a fairly short time the new government, probably using German reparations payments, rebuilt the houses of Vižovlje. Once again the hamlet in which Franc would live and raise his family looked much as it had when Franc's great-great-grandfather Tomaž had moved there more than a century earlier. Just as then, fourteen rough fieldstone houses and barns clustered around the point where one dirt road parted from another, only now all the houses had tile roofs, and they had been rebuilt without the picturesque chimney kitchens.[14] Once again, shabbily dressed farmers maneuvered their ox carts on the manure-strewn roads and their kerchiefed wives drove cows to pasture or carried bundles of sticks on their heads. In 1929 a guidebook for hikers and climbers in the Karst referred in passing to Vižovlje and Mavhinje as "poor farming places, where there is nothing but some primitive tavern."[15]

When Franc returned from the war he resumed his former place on the farm-to-factory continuum. He continued to work in towns, on country roads, or in quarries, but he lived in Vižovlje because he could not imagine living anywhere else but in this tiny hamlet of weatherbeaten farmers and laborers. Having made this decision, it was also natural to conclude that he would have to make his living just as he had done before the war, by taking any job that came his way. Before long he was working for a local contractor repairing the badly war-damaged roads of the Karst and building new ones.

Fig. 13. Sardine plant workers at Duino, about 1914. *Lojza Kočjančič, who later married Franc Žužek, is the young woman on the far left, nearest to the foreman.*

As we have seen, even before the war Franc had planned to marry, but his fiancée had changed her mind. Now he was a man in his thirties, on his own, employed, and the owner of a small house. The time had passed when parents chose their children's spouses. In any case, Franc's father was dead and his mother (next door to Valentin's house) was probably indifferent to what he did. Franc could marry or not as he chose, and he could marry whom he chose.

One day he was walking home from work in Monfalcone when he came upon a middle-aged couple and a young woman struggling to right an overturned hay wagon. The couple were Ivan Kočjančič (*coach yan' chich*), a farmer and quarry worker and sometimes silkworm raiser from nearby Cerovlje, and his wife Lojza (*loy' za*). The young woman was their daughter, who was also named Lojza. She was a tall, plump, black-haired young woman, some eight years younger than Franc. Like Franc, Lojza had experienced some of the transition to industrialism. As a girl she had gone to school in Mavhinje until she was fourteen and also worked in various ways to add to her family's income. While still very small she carried milk every day from Cerovlje to a few houses in Sistiana, one of these being the seaside home of some cousins of the prince of Duino. Later she and her parents worked at home producing silk-worm cocoons for a manufacturer in Friuli. Still later she found work in a small sardine-processing plant in Duino. Here, in a large house at the base of the cliffs below the castle, she and fifty other women cleaned sardines and then either canned them or dried and salted them and packed them in barrels. *

Work in this processing plant must have been closer to the experience of disciplined, regimented industrial labor than anything women on the Karst had ever known, and they were made to work hard. The eleven-hour workday began promptly at 6:00 A.M., and lateness was not tolerated. The process of cleaning fish and then either canning them or frying, salting, and packing them in barrels was not carried out in assembly-line fashion. Rather, all the women completed one stage of the work together and then turned to the next stage. At noon they had an hour's lunch break, during which they ate the boiled eggs or cooked dried beans they had brought from home or the sardines they had filched during the morning. Then they worked on from 1:00 to 6:00 P.M. *

Thus Lojza, like Franc, had grown up in a farm village and still lived there, but she nevertheless had some experience of the industrial world. Like him, she also knew something of war. Repeatedly, between 1915 and 1918, her family had been driven from their hamlet by Italian shelling, and they had spent long periods living as refugees in friends' sheds in hamlets farther from the front. For a while they supported themselves, as others did, by pounding rocks into gravel, which Austro-Hungarian soldiers then spread on the country roads to make them passable for trucks and ammunition caissons. Once Lojza almost died of typhus.

But to return to Franc's first meeting with Lojza, Franc helped the Kočjančič family to right their wagon and reload their hay, and he also decided that he would go to Cerovlje later and call on Lojza. Before long the two were engaged,

---

* A literary footnote: the German poet Rainer Maria Rilke spent the winter of 1911–12 as a guest in the castle of Duino. One violently windy day he went out and paced to and fro along the bastions with the sea raging two hundred feet below. Suddenly, according to his translator (Rilke 1939: 10), he stopped, because it seemed that from the midst of the storm a voice had called to him: "Who, if I cried, would hear me among the angelic orders?" This would be the opening line of his most celebrated work, *Duino Elegies*. As inspiration came to the poet, Lojza was probably down below in the factory at the base of the cliffs cleaning, salting, or frying sardines.

* My source is Emma Pahor of Sistiana. She and her sister both worked in the sardine plant while Lojza did, but their home was in Jamlje (*yam' lyeh*), which is considerably farther from Duino than Cerovlje. They rose each day at 3:30 A.M., dressed and ate, and then walked barefoot to the plant, putting on their sandals of coiled rags only where the road was especially rough. In the evening they got home at eight. If boyfriends were waiting for them, their mother would meet them at the edge of Jamlje and warn them to run to the village cistern and wash off the smell of fish before they came to the house.

although this did not happen without a snag. Cerovlje was one of two nearby Karst hamlets with strong traditions of endogamous marriage; the young men and women customarily married others from the same village.[16] An outsider who wished to marry a girl from Cerovlje sometimes had to fight some of the young men of the village before they would allow him to set foot there. In the case of Franc (who after all was a tough war veteran in his mid-thirties) this formality was waived after he had stood all the young men of Cerovlje to drinks in the local tavern. He and Lojza were married in October 1922.

His marriage to a local woman from a family of farmers and laborers probably confirmed Franc in his decision to stay in his native hamlet and make his living as a laborer. He would never waver from it in the nearly six more decades of life ahead of him. These decades would not be easy, as we shall see, but he seems to have been contented with his lot.

At the beginning of this chapter, we asked how Franc and Emil Žužek would fare as they tried to find places for themselves in an industrializing world. In some respects their experiences were similar. The brothers had been influenced by the same general social forces. They had probably survived infancy and childhood as the lucky beneficiaries of the widespread decline in child mortality. In the cause of modernization, the Austro-Hungarian government had provided them with formal schooling. They had fought in a world war. They had had to make their way in a society undergoing an industrial revolution. They belonged to a great emerging proletariat.

The courses of their lives were very different, however. Emil left home, wandered from place to place, and slowly disintegrated. Did he fail in life because he was a displaced person, helpless in the face of the changes brought about by those general social forces? Did he drink, beat his children, and wander aimlessly because he was a farm boy and a Slovene *Untermensch* who could not adjust to the realities of urban industrial life? Quite possibly. On the other hand, Franc too had had to find a place, a slot to fill in an industrializing world. He had had to make roughly the same adjustment and had done it in a very different way. Unlike Emil he managed a happy compromise. Not only did he remain in his native hamlet while he held jobs in the developing industrial economy, becoming an amphibian at home in two worlds; as we shall see, he also developed the values and attitudes he needed for his place in life. His adaptability and good sense helped him to manage with considerable ease the adjustment that Emil so disastrously failed to make.

8

Becoming Modern

One summer evening during the 1920s Franc Žužek approached his employer at the marble quarry in Nabrežina after work. We can imagine how Franc looked: a short, wiry, deeply tanned man with dark, curly hair, his shabby clothes covered with gray powder (see Fig. 15). "I would like to talk about my pay," he said respectfully. "It is very little." "Oh," said his boss, "would nothing be better?"

In later life Franc Žužek often told that little story, which illustrates the precariousness of his family's existence in the interwar period. In this chapter we will be concerned with that vulnerability and with Franc and Lojza's reactions to it. We will see how in order to survive and prosper they dropped old ways and adopted new ones. To use a term usually applied to whole societies, not individuals, they "modernized." They became the kind of people they had to be.[1]

In his efforts to survive as a village laborer in the industrial economy Franc enjoyed certain advantages. He had a tough body and a resilient spirit, he enjoyed a reputation as a good worker and a likable fellow, he owned a small house, and he was married to a capable woman who already knew something about survival in that border area between the old subsistence farming and the new industrialism.

Italy, when it took over Trieste and the Karst after World War I, promised its new citizens a better life. "Slovenes!" declared the Italian governor general in a proclamation posted on the walls in towns and villages, "The Italian and Slovene peoples are no longer enemies. . . . Today the two peoples can divide the work and the profits. Italy today is counted among the great European powers because it possesses great industries built by it in recent years with its own efforts [and] because it has a well developed foreign trade and agriculture and a high level of culture. Only a great industrial and commercial force like Italy can assure you the well-being you need."[2]

The economic prediction proved false, however. Trieste, which normally was the major provider of jobs for the Karst, gained little from linking up with the industrialized economy of northern Italy. On the contrary, its trade and industries suffered from the fact that the vast Hapsburg empire, for which the city had formerly served as a port, had now been divided into small nations,[3] and these nations tended to use other ports. In addition, the whole industrialized world would suffer from the depression of the late 1920s and 1930s.

The economic problems were not all that made life in these years difficult. The new Italian government fairly quickly proved to be a harsh one. This too was not what had been promised. The Italian governor general who had proclaimed that Italy would bring prosperity to the Karst had also declared that "Italy, this great nation of liberty, today gives you schools in your own language, [which is] more than Austria gave you. . . . Slovenes, rest assured that great and victorious Italy looks after its citizens within its new borders without regard to their nationality."[4]

Again, it was not to be so. Early in the 1920s, when Mussolini became the dictator of Italy, Fascist authorities in the Slovene-speaking area of Italy quickly set about Italianizing their subjects.[5] They required that all Slovene children be taught solely in Italian, they censored Slovene books, and they changed not only place names but even family and personal names to Italian ones.[6] The Žužeks now had to write their last name according to Italian spelling rules—Susech—and Lojza's family name was changed from Kočjančič to Canciani. As their younger children were born, late in the decade, Franc and Lojza surrendered to the inescapable and gave them Italian first names: Angelo, Elda, and Nerina. Local officials often carried out the Italianization process quite brutally. An Italian Fascist in a butcher shop in Sistiana heard nine-year-old Maks Kočjančič, Lojza Žužek's nephew, address the Slovene butcher in their own language. "I'll teach you to use that Slav language," he said, and struck Maks's head so hard that blood flowed from his mouth. *

What was just as important as the attack on Slovene ethnicity was the exclusion of Slovenes from good jobs. Under Mussolini the best posts went to Fascists, most of whom were Italians. As Franc would later say, no Fascists

---

* Kočjančič says that when he happened to meet the same man in a nearby bar years later, when he himself was full grown and husky, he lifted him off the ground and "shook him a little."

worked down in the quarry pits. The combination of repression and depression contributed to the emigration from the Italian border territory of some one hundred thousand Croats and Slovenes during the 1920s and 1930s. Some went across the border to Yugoslavia, others to northwestern Europe, others across the Atlantic to South America.[7]

Why were the local Fascists so hard on the people of the Karst?[8] Many Italians, and perhaps most Triestines, claimed that the Slovenes were "primitive and uneducated peoples, . . . the last who came to the civilized commonwealth of Europe."[9] Some of them viewed—or claimed to view—forced Italianization as a favor to the Slovenes, a way of integrating them into a higher culture and a more developed economy. More of them, probably, saw it as a favor to themselves, a way to achieve a more perfect Italian ethnic unity and safer borders with Austria and Yugoslavia.[10] But why did the Fascist authorities Italianize so harshly, and why did they also practice or permit job discrimination? In reality, it seems that fascism in the Trieste area simply accommodated itself to the traditional use of the Slovenes as an under class. This will surprise no one who is aware that many historians have seen European fascism as an ideology of the dominant classes, invented to help them hold on to their own social positions.[11] Some Slovene historians claim that Italians in and near Trieste adopted fascism especially eagerly because it provided an outlook that was useful in coping with the slowly rising aspirations of the nearby Slovene and Croatian under classes.[12]

Despite all the obstacles, in the two decades between the world wars Franc Žužek was almost never without work. For the first two years after his return from World War I he worked for a road-building company. At first he worked with a pick and shovel, but later he drove a steamroller, a machine whose harnessed energy was virtually the symbol of the industrialization process that was slowly transforming life on the Karst. He helped to carve out the "new road" that descends dramatically to Trieste from the northwest along the seaside cliffs. Then he found a job making roads in the Istrian Peninsula for another construction company, again driving a gigantic steam roller. He took a room in the town of Portoroz and came home for visits when he could. For a while he worked in the shipyard in Monfalcone where before the war he had driven a team of horses. Then he found work once again in the quarries at Nabrežina and stayed there for five years. Much of this time it was his task to pour sand and water under a long saw wire powered by a steam engine. And these were only some of the jobs he held in these two decades. Jobs—humble, poorly paid ones—were available for a man with a reputation as a good worker, and this continued to be true even in the Great Depression. Indeed,

Franc seems to have scarcely been aware that he lived through that great economic crisis.

In any case, the work was always hard and dangerous. In the period of five
years when Franc worked in the quarries at Nabrežina, five men who worked
with him were killed in accidents. He recalled three of these deaths vividly: a
block of marble fell on one man; machinery clutched the coat of another and
smashed him against a wall; a third entered a crack or vein in the marble
carrying TNT while smoking, and the explosive ignited and burned him to
death. The work was also poorly paid, because there was an abundance of
farmers' sons, all with about the same level of skills, ready and eager to do the
same work.

The conditions in which Franc and Lojza now lived were both better and
worse than those that they had known as children. Their status as members of
an under class had certainly not risen and may even have fallen as a result of
the government's attacks on Slovene culture. They did enjoy some new public
services, however, because the government, the same one that sought so
harshly to Italianize them, was also in various modest ways improving the
quality of life on the Karst. By the late 1930s water was piped to a pump on
the lower side of Vižovlje, a new train station (for the benefit of vacationers
headed for the seashore a mile away) had replaced the old one, and a new
one-room school near the hamlet had replaced the smaller and more distant
one in Mavhinje. Meanwhile, their material standard of living, which we will
examine more fully in the next chapter, was somewhat higher than it had
been a generation earlier. Even so, food was still limited, clothing inade-
quate, medicine primitive, life hard. In 1929 the parish priest in Mavhinje
wrote in his report to his bishop that the economic condition of his parish-
ioners in Vižovlje, Cerovlje, and Mavhinje was "pessimus."[13]

Emigration might have provided an alternative to the Žužeks' fairly hard
lot. Even before the war some of Franc's friends had left the Karst, embarked
on ships at Trieste, and traveled in steerage class to North or South America.
They had found work as lumberjacks in Minnesota, steelworkers in Cleveland
and Pittsburgh, and laborers in Buenos Aires.[14] Like so many others in the
Western world's industrial work force they were circulating in a great human
bloodstream. During the 1920s Franc and Lojza considered the possibility of
emigrating to "America" (a word used vaguely to refer to the two continents),
staying long enough to save some money, and then returning. Lojza was fairly
enthusiastic about the idea, but her husband loved his home, his way of life,
and the Karst, and there they stayed.

If he had to stay in the Karst, then, but found it hard to survive, there was a way for a man like Franc to raise his income: he could moonlight in crime. Others sometimes did it; so, conceivably, might he. Local views of what kind of activity was criminal were complex. Poaching to feed one's family, for instance, was viewed by people on the Karst as acceptable behavior. A man might slip into the publicly-owned woods, as Franc did from time to time, to trap hares with wire-loop snares, and no one would look down on him for it. When the local game warden, his neighbor Anton Klarič,[15] caught Franc in the woods with a dead hare he had trapped, he fined him but remained his friend. Poaching was not a violation of the moral code; it was just a way to feed one's family and a game one played with the authorities.

A Karst farmer or laborer would almost never steal from a neighbor, however, or even from a family in another hamlet. For one thing, it was too risky; he might be caught. For another, his victim would be a person like him, a fellow man who was struggling to get by. One could never stoop so low as to steal a bicycle leaning against a barn in a village. Only vagabonds and gypsies from the outside world did that.

Stealing from those who were rich and distant, however, was another matter, listed in a different section of the moral code book and subject to varying interpretations. During the 1920s some of Franc's friends, men from nearby hamlets whom he had known since childhood, became part-time thieves, and once they tried to involve Franc with them. They had formed a plan to steal not from their neighbors but from distant victims. They knew that trains headed toward Trieste had to climb a slight grade near Vižovlje. Their plan was to grease or soap the railroad tracks at this point, so that as a freight train climbed the grade it would slip and come almost to a halt. They would then climb into the cars and take what they could find. Since they knew that Franc was an agile man and could use money to support his growing family, they urged him to take part. Franc refused. His views on this kind of theft were different from theirs, and he was smarter. His friends went ahead with their plan, but they were caught by the police and spent several years in prison.

To sum up what we have been saying thus far in this chapter, Franc and Lojza in effect chose in the 1920s to live out their lives on the Karst and to depend mainly on what Franc could earn in honest ways as a laborer. At the very least their goal was to survive, and they were as well equipped to do this as the next family. Probably they aimed not merely to survive but to continue that small rise in living standards that both had witnessed in their youth, before the war, and that governments like Italy were leading their people to expect would continue.

Survival, and especially a continued rise in living standards, would depend on many things, some of which were beyond their control. But one thing Franc and Lojza could do, and would have to do, was to change the views and the ways of living they had learned from their parents and grandparents. They would have to modernize.

The term *modernization* means different things to different people. To an American anthropologist who has studied the changing life of peasants in the northern Andes mountains, modernization is "the process by which individuals change from a traditional way of life to a more complex, technologically advanced, and rapidly changing style of life." Many social scientists now use the word in that sense, stressing the ways in which individuals change their ways and their views as they become modern.[16] We shall use the term modernization that way here as we look at the way Franc and Lojza adopted new attitudes and new kinds of behavior during the 1920s and 1930s. We do not say that they were the first Žužeks to adopt new ways; we have already discussed some adaptations made by earlier Žužeks. We do say that for this couple in these decades our information is more plentiful, and we can now look more closely at changing ideas and behavior. We shall see how this couple were becoming modern people.

One of the first decisions these two must have had to make after their marriage was how to divide the work. Both were familiar with the male/female division of labor as their parents (themselves involved in social transition) had practiced it. The man, a farmer and part-time carter or quarryman, had worked both on and away from the farm and had earned most of his family's income. His wife did the household chores and the farm work that her husband lacked the time to do. For Franc and Lojza, however, things were in some ways quite different, because as a full-time laborer Franc was away not for short periods but all day, six days a week; sometimes, in fact, he was away for weeks at a time. Franc therefore adoped this routine: he rose at dawn, hauled water from one of the village cisterns or the new pump and watered the vegetables, fed the pig he kept in a pen beside the house,[17] ate a breakfast consisting of bread chunks soaked in barley "coffee" and milk, and walked off to work. When he returned in the evening he was likely to weed his garden, slip into the woods and set a snare (for a hare), eat his supper, shoo his chickens up to their sleeping roosts, and then follow their example.

Lojza's daily routine included most of the traditional tasks that made up women's work, and some of the chores near the house that Franc lacked the time to do. Usually she rose later than Franc. While he was at work she cooked and cleaned, fed the chickens, and, if Franc was not employed too far away, made his lunch and took it to him.[18] She bought what food the Žužeks could not produce in their garden from itinerant vendors or at a store in Sistiana. She also sewed clothes, patched and darned them, washed them with water drawn sparingly from the cisterns, and sometimes lugged them for miles to the Timavo River to rinse out the soap. Once a week she baked bread in the stone oven by the side of the house. All of these were typical women's chores, but to make up for the loss of Franc's presence she also did some of the tasks that were more properly done by men, such as cutting wood in the Vižovlje common and carrying it home, and helping to tend the vegetable garden. When the children were old enough to permit it, she sometimes walked some two hours to the remote hamlet of Samatorca to help her widowed sister Neta with her farm work and then trudged home at dusk. Franc and the children would walk part way along the rocky road to meet her, hallooing through the darkness until she hallooed back, and then meeting her and walking back together to Vižovlje.

What happened, then, in no very dramatic way, was that Franc and Lojza made some significant changes in the family division of labor. To accommodate himself to an industrializing society in which the best-paid jobs went to men, Franc concentrated on working at laboring jobs away from home, although he still did many chores at home in his spare time. Lojza meanwhile had taken over some of his gardening and other chores. Millions of village laborers' wives must have taken over some light farming chores in similar fashion; this was quite the opposite of what blue collar workers' wives were doing in the towns and cities. (These women were often doing less economically productive work than their grandmothers and mothers had done as farm wives. They concentrated instead on managing households and trying to steer their husbands and children away from crime and alcohol.[19]) Lojza also had to take over more of the supervision of the children, something we shall discuss more fully later on. In short, Franc and Lojza had modernized their division of the workload in such a way as to profit as much as they could from the developing economy.

Modernization involves attitudes as well as behavior, particularly attitudes about work. Franc would have to modernize his thinking about his job and internalize the values needed for economic development. We have earlier recounted two anecdotes about him that suggest that he had already shown himself to be a person who was receptive to new ways. When as a teen-ager he had admired the dashing English engineers at the shipyard where he worked and had bought a pipe and tried to smoke as they did, he was in effect trying to modernize, to pattern himself on the new and successful. When, not long after that, a salesman persuaded him to buy that newfangled invention, a bicycle, and to pay for it in installments, he showed himself a person who could move with the times.

In furnishing his mind with ideas about life and work, Franc chose some very old furniture. Chief among these ideas was the doctrine that we should simply resign ourselves to whatever God has ordained. No doubt he had absorbed this idea from his parents and from the sermons of priests at Mavhinje. It was a conservative belief, suitable for his humble peasant ancestors and good enough, too, for a humble laborer.

Franc also believed in an optimistic corollary to the basic proposition that we must accept what God has ordained for us. He was convinced that each of us is born, indeed destined, to do a certain kind of work. This is also an ancient notion, at least as old as the medieval view that God ordained that there be those who fought, those who labored, and those who prayed. Franc merely added some refinements to that ancient division to allow for more specialized trades. A carpenter, to him, was a person who was more or less intended by God to work with wood, a plumber was intended to control the flow of water through pipes, a farmer to tend animals and grow crops, a merchant to sell, a doctor to heal. Each was intended to do what he did, and usually he did it well, or at least he should aim to. Franc's own trade was the generalized one of laborer, which meant that he had mastered a few simple skills such as handling horses, swiftly shoveling sand, cement, and water together to make concrete, carving postholes in the Karst rock with a sledge hammer and cold chisel, and shaping wooden handles for his tools. Having pride in his own skills, he admired those of men in other lines of work, men who had been destined to do other things and who did them well. It gave him pleasure to watch a mason build a stone wall with the barest minimum of mortar between the stones or a ceramist carefully prepare a wall and then quickly cover it with precisely placed tiles.

And yet even if God had foreordained what each of us should do, there was certainly nothing sacred about the calling. One might take pride in one's skills, enjoy the companionship of other workmen, sometimes even enjoy the work itself, but it was only work, and a job was only a job. For this reason Franc was able to move from one laboring job to another, aiming mainly to support a family, seeking higher pay if possible but paying no regard to the inherent interest of the work. For him what made one job better than another was, first, better pay and job security, and second, less dirt and less exposure to bad weather. As far as dirt and exposure were concerned, farming was worst, and laboring slightly better. An ideal position was that of the post office clerk or salesperson, for their hands were clean and they were never burned by the sun or frozen by the bora.

In short, then, Franc's views and attitudes about work were both old and new. His resignation to hardships and his belief that each of us was predestined to do a certain kind of work were ancient attitudes but well adapted to the needs of a humble laborer on the Karst. On the other hand, he was quite willing to pick up new ways: to buy a bicycle, purchase on the installment plan if necessary, put his money in a savings bank, drive a steamroller. His matter-of-fact attitude that a job is a job was a fairly new outlook, which perhaps contradicted his own view that God had destined us to do certain kinds of work. It helped him to adjust to both layoffs and new jobs, and it made him a useful movable part in the fluid industrial system, an all-purpose what's-it who could fill in wherever needed.

Franc and Lojza also modernized their reproductive behavior. They seem to have been transitional figures in the limiting of family size (see Table 7).

As baby makers, earlier generations of Žužeks had been very energetic: they produced a lot and kept at the job for a long time. At the start of the nineteenth century, as we saw, Tomaž and Marina Žužek had married young, produced eleven children, and might have had more if Marina had not died soon after bearing the last child at the age of thirty-six. Matija and his wife married young and had a dozen children; when the last was born, Marijana was forty-two. At midcentury Jožef[1] and his wife married young and had nine children, with the last born when Frančiška was forty-one. Late in the century Jožef[II] and his wife Marija married young and had eight children, of which the last was born when Marija was forty-four.

In the early twentieth century, however, Franc and Lojza seem to have followed a different pattern, one that historical demographers have often ob-

---

TABLE 7
Children of Franc (1888–1978) and Lojza (1896–1976)

	DATES	CAUSE OF DEATH
Berta	1923–	
Vida	1926–	
Angelo	1927–	
Elda	1930–	[twin]
Nerina	1930–31	[twin] "weakness"

served in the birth records of groups of people who have reduced their marital fertility. In this new behavior pattern, married couples no longer keep producing children until the wives cease to be fecund. Instead they have children at a fairly rapid rate early in the marriage and then, long before the wives can no longer conceive, they stop. Indeed, demographers sometimes call the new pattern "stopping behavior." Just how couples stopped before the advent of modern means of contraception is not clear. Suffice it to say that where there was a will there was a way.

In any case, with Franc and Lojza we can see the new pattern. Married in 1922, they had a child at the end of 1923, a second twenty-six months later, another fourteen months after that, and twins after another thirty-one months. Lojza nursed her children. (In fact, for a few months during 1930–31 she is said to have nursed four babies—her own twins and the twins of a mother who could not produce enough milk for her own children.) Since the first three children all survived infancy, she nursed them for many months, and this fact accounts for the fairly long intervals between births. Up to now she had followed the traditional reproductive pattern. She and Franc now had five children, the result of four pregnancies. But after the birth of the twins and after she had ceased to nurse them, she bore no more children. Lojza was only thirty-five and perhaps she could have conceived children for nearly another decade. Possibly she was now sterile, but it seems more likely that she and Franc deliberately stopped.

If so, Franc and Lojza were behaving like millions of other couples who reduced their fertility during the nineteenth and twentieth centuries.[20] Birthrates everywhere were dropping, first in the cities and among the middle and upper classes, later among the poor and in the countryside. This trend was quite visible in Trieste and its hinterland. In the early 1900s, married couples in the Karst still produced nearly twice as many children as couples in Trieste, but country and city people alike were sharply reducing the number of their children.[21]

Reducing fertility was a response to social change. A student of the population history of the Trieste area has guessed that those who reduced their fertility did so partly because they realized that infant mortality was dropping and that they did not have to produce many children in the hope that a few would survive. But these couples probably also wanted to avoid the expense of having numerous children in order to maintain their own improved standard of living, and they wanted to give their children the expensive upbringing and education that they needed if they too were to prosper.[22]

These motives and others as well probably influenced Franc and Lojza.

They may have been vaguely aware of the decline in the infant mortality rate that is so apparent when one looks at the Žužek generations in the nineteenth century (see Table 5), and they may also have had a sense that life had improved somewhat for them and could be even better for their children if they could limit their number. As country people who did not farm, they may have reflected that Franc would never need sons to take over any farm work from him. We should also keep in mind that Franc and Lojza belonged to the first generation on the Karst that was almost universally able to read. That fact may have had something to do with their "stopping behavior." As people who could read, Franc and Lojza were more likely to absorb the values of a modernizing society and to realize that their contemporaries were having fewer children. Rising literacy is often associated with a decline in fertility.[23]

Just as Franc had taken old beliefs and mixed them with new experiences to come up with a useful view of work, so he also seems to have taken over and reshaped a view of family life that was suited to the life of a village laborer. In earlier generations, the head of the Žužek family had been an authoritarian figure who commanded his wife, and even more his children, as if he were an admiral and they common seamen. By 1930 things were different. Franc's work was unlike that of his farmer ancestors. As a laborer he was away for much of the day and sometimes for weeks at a time.[24] Lojza therefore took up some of the burden of authority. Partly as a result of this new division of power and partly because they were reasonable people, the two lived on equal terms. They were partners in the running of the household.

In the meantime, since they were not the managers of a subsistence farm, their relations with their children were also different from those of earlier generations. Franc and Lojza could not, as their forefathers had done, demand hard work of their children, since such work was not clearly, urgently needed for bare survival. They could not command the same degree of respect that children formerly paid to parents when the older generation had skills that the children had to learn if they were to survive. And they could not so effectively threaten a disobedient son with disinheritance, since they had no farmland to leave him, and he was bound to realize early in life that what would count most in his future would not be land but his own skills and knowledge.

This is not to say that Franc and Lojza had no sway over their offspring. Their older children, especially Berta, the firstborn, remember them as having often been strict. She recalls that for smaller offenses Lojza might slap them, and for bigger ones Franc would beat them with a stick "all over." On one occasion when they were talking with neighbors, Franc had the impression that Berta was laughing at him. When they were alone he picked up a long stick and chased her. Berta managed to escape and all day stayed away from home, but when she returned that night and sneaked into the bedroom the three sisters shared, he came in and gave her the beating she had tried to avoid. Today Berta believes she understands the reasons for her parents' strictness. Their own lives were hard, she says, and they had much to worry about. Moreover, her mother was often exhausted from her hard physical work, and when her older children were teenagers she was in menopause.

Franc and Lojza never insisted that the children be silent or vanish when there were other adults present—that silence that betokened total respect and obedience. In later years the two parents seem to have been very mild disciplinarians for their two younger children (one of the twins, Nerina, had died in infancy). Unlike the older two, Angelo and Elda grew up addressing their parents with the informal *ti* (you) rather than with the formal *vi*, which conveys greater distance and respect. By 1940, if not sooner, Franc seems to have completely abandoned the stern parental style that he had known as a boy. Perhaps he had realized that such strictness was better suited to a farm family with very scarce means than to the family of a village laborer in a more complex economy.

Franc and Lojza had to prepare their children to survive in an evolving, slowly industrializing economy. No longer was it enough for a father to teach his son to yoke an ox, sickle hay, build a wall, or prune a vine, or for a mother to teach her daughter to milk a cow, clean a fish, gather herbs, or darn a shirt. Children who were to live in a modernized economy might have to read blueprints, make change, keep accounts, or type letters. For over four decades, attendance at elementary school had already been required by law on the Karst, and Franc and Lojza had themselves learned to read and write and do sums. Now that was no longer enough. The two parents would have to decide how much formal schooling their children needed.

At first Berta, and then Vida, Angelo, and Elda attended the new little school in Vižovlje. The Italian schoolmistress was considerably gentler than the rod wielder their parents had known, although she was strict enough about fining them if they spoke in their native tongue. Even in their elementary-school years the children began to be prepared for different sex roles. The boys began to learn mechanical drawing, while the girls learned to embroider towels and blouses. After school, other organizatons helped to shape the children. Once a week they walked to Mavhinje, where the priest instructed them in Catholic doctrine and also clandestinely taught them to read and write a little in the Slovene language. All four were enrolled in Fascist youth organizations, Angelo becoming a "Son of the She-Wolf" at the age of four and later joining the Balilla, and the girls becoming "Piccole Italiane," or Little Italians. In the summers, government-run day camps took the children off their parents' hands for a few hours a day.

School, church, and party together did not take up more than half of the children's waking hours, however. They also had chores to do at home, and for the girls these came to include the weekly relentless scrubbing of the bare wood floors of the entire house. Sometimes they helped neighborhood children to take their cows to pasture, and Elda pastured the Žužeks' white goat by walking her on a leash and letting her graze by the roadside. The girls also began to buy linen for their hope chests and to embroider each piece with floral patterns and their initials. In spring they picked wild asparagus in the woods and brought it home to be cooked for dinner, and on summer weekends they picked bunches of pink cyclamens and took them to the station to sell to passengers on the trains. Sometimes the children of Vižovlje and nearby villages played epic games of hide-and-seek over miles of fields and woods.

As far as their son was concerned, Franc and Lojza understood very well

Fig. 14. Vida Žužek (facing front) in government-run day camp, mid-1930s.

the need for an education that would prepare him to do skilled work. When Angelo had finished elementary school near Vižovlje, they encouraged him to begin the equivalent of high school in Nabrežina. (World War II later prevented his completing it.) For boys this school placed a heavy emphasis on instruction in drafting, and in later years Angelo put this skill to use when he worked as a welder.

Franc and Lojza took their three daughters' schooling much less seriously. Like most Slovenes, and indeed most blue-collar Europeans, they looked at girls as future housewives who did not need much in the way of formal education. Industrialization had not yet changed this view very much in the Karst, and most Slovene women still entered the labor market as unskilled and almost unschooled workers. True, during the 1920s and 1930s, just as the Žužek girls began their schooling, the educational gap was closing. A higher percentage of Slovene girls began attending secondary schools and even universities,[25] but this happened mainly to those in and near the city.

When Berta and Vida had completed the elementary-school grades in Vižovlje, their parents did not send them to high school in Nabrežina, as they were to do with Angelo. "After all," Vida would say wryly in later years, "he was a boy." Essentially, therefore, the girls learned to be superior housewives, not wage earners. Armed with only elementary-school educations, the housewifely arts that they had learned from their mother, and a superb command of embroidery, they were poorly equipped to earn their livings in a developing economy. At an early age Berta left home to become a live-in maid in Nabrežina, and Vida later followed in her footsteps. Their parents would urge them to become sales clerks, but this was not an easy jump to make. (Vida would later make that change.) Perhaps Elda might have stayed in school longer than her sisters, but for her great events would rule out an education relevant to modern economic life. World War II totally disrupted the Žužeks' lives and stopped her schooling when she was fourteen years old.

By the eve of World War II, Franc and Lojza clearly had adopted views and ways of life that fitted in well with the general process of industrialization. In other words, they had modernized. True, their grandparents and parents before them had also modernized in some respects. True also, their descendants would continue to do the same. But consider how much these two had done in a couple of decades. Franc had adopted the attitudes about work that were useful for a blue-collar worker in a fluid labor force. Lojza and he had shaped a division of power and labor suitable for a household in which the husband was away during much of the day. They had produced a number of children more

Fig. 15. Franc Žužek in about 1940. *An identity card photograph.*

appropriate than the big outputs of earlier generations for an age of reduced infant mortality and for a family that had no need for its children's labor. They were raising their children with less of the stern discipline that had been natural to the bygone age of real want. They were even seeing that their children got some of the formal schooling they would need.

Suggestions of the new modernized man can be found in a photograph of Franc, which was taken when he was about half a century old (Fig. 15). The very fact that he posed for an identification card picture like this one tells us that Franc had adjusted to the demands of a society more complex and regimented than any his ancestors had known. In this picture he wears an ill-tied necktie, which was probably his only one, since he was almost never known to wear one, even with his Sunday suit. He wears it because he knows it is what a man now wears on this kind of occasion. On his face is an expression that says, "I know I have to do this, so here I am."

9

Costs of War

Kerosene and matches on a hot summer day in 1944 would shed some light on this question: what could modern war do to the gains that had been made by families like the Žužeks?

While many lost their lives in World War II, many others who escaped death or injury nevertheless suffered terrible hardships and economic losses. Sometimes during World War II the industrialized nations deliberately aimed to destroy their enemies' economies by blowing up their factories, their railroads, their docks, and their airports.[1] Even when the belligerents had no such deliberate economic strategy, the results were often the same. Bombs, shortages, insecurity, and the deaths of productive people all combined to disrupt production, lower living standards, and destroy public services and utilities.[2] In Italy, for example, the war destroyed two-fifths of the schools, more than half the roads, more than half of the merchant ships, and some two million habitable rooms. Between 1938 and 1945 the national income (all the earnings of labor and property) fell by more than half. By 1945 the average Italian was spending more than a third less, in real terms, than he had in 1940. He was eating a lot less.[3] I emphatically do not mean to say that the economic effects of the war were as horrible as the terror, maiming, sorrow, and death, and in fact I shall have something to say about these in this chapter. My main concern, however, will be with the experience of the war's economic and social effects. How would the village laborer Franc Žužek and his family cope with the calamity of war? How would the living standard of a family that had only recently risen from real poverty bear up in the general chaos? Would the Žužeks, like rural people in some other countries, fare somewhat better in the war than city dwellers?[4]

In order to answer these questions we must first establish just how well the Žužeks did in fact live in the decade just before the war. In the 1930s, then, when Franc and Lojza were middle-aged, their children were very young, and laboring jobs were poorly paid, what did the Žužeks eat? A typical meal, especially for the children, consisted of potato or bean soup and the black bread that Lojza baked once a week. Often there was cornmeal mush instead of bread, and a vegetable from the large garden behind the house. Occasionally all ate meat or chicken, but as in the past, the rule was that adults, and especially men, needed more animal protein in their diet than children.[5] Franc's daughter Berta remembers being sent by her mother to take her father his lunch at a quarry in Sistiana where he worked for a while. En route she looked in the box and saw that it contained some bread, some green beans, and a fried egg. She was hungry and could not resist tasting the egg again and again. By the time she reached her father, the egg had disappeared. When he opened the box and gathered what had happened, Franc only shook his head in mock perplexity.

Nevertheless, with his garden and his earnings as a laborer, Franc could feed his children better than his parents had fed their children a generation earlier. To some extent the family's diet had also been gradually enriched over perhaps half a century by new vegetables that had made their way east from Italy. These included broccoli, chicory, tomatoes, and carrots. Especially useful was the bland green plant called corn salad, which grows well in early spring or late fall and extended the months in which the family had green vegetables. These plants and others added both vitamins and variety to the diet. Meanwhile their schoolteacher gave the children a spoonful of cod-liver oil each day as part of a government program to prevent rickets. To the Žužek children, starved for animal fats, cod-liver oil was something to look forward to with pleasure.

The Žužeks now lived in a house with more living space than the homes that Franc and Lojza had known as children. Not that the house was larger, for it was not, but there were fewer children to crowd into it, and then, too, Franc had converted the first-floor stable into a bedroom. Their furnishings may have been a little more comfortable. Franc and Lojza had bought themselves a wool-stuffed mattress, something neither had ever had before. Berta, Angelo, and Elda slept on homemade corn-shuck mattresses, but Vida had a wool mattress that Lojza's mother had bought for herself in her old age and then bequeathed to this favorite grandchild.

Meanwhile their lives were being enriched by the arrival of public utilities and services. The national and local governments laid pipes across the Karst and brought water to public pumps in Vižovlje. It was probably this water that made possible the Žužeks' large garden and the vegetables that enriched their diet. A telephone line connected the Vižovlje train station to others and could be used in an emergency to call a doctor. Roads were improved, and these made it easier for Franc to ride his old bicycle to work at Sistiana or Nabrežina and for vendors to reach the hamlet with oranges and other fruit and smelts and sea bass. Perhaps most important of all, the government built the one-room elementary school on the edge of Vižovlje that we have already mentioned. Here it was that the teacher fed the children their mixture of the three Rs, propaganda, and cod-liver oil.

Although the improvements in their diet probably made the Žužek children healthier than children of their parents' generation, their lack of means nevertheless stood between them and professional medical care. Only very rarely did they see a doctor. Instead Lojza treated her children's ills with a combination of homemade medicines, prayer, psychology, magic, and humor. She rubbed cuts and bruises with herbs she had gathered in the fields, or with rancid butter made from the creamy milk that her neighbors' cows gave in May when the pasture grass was thick, or with the melted and strained fat of hedgehogs. She put vinegar compresses on the children's brows when they suffered from headaches. For various kinds of muscle pains she had the children stand near a cabinet while she opened and closed its door and recited an incantation. When their stomachs ached, she told them to slide down the stairs headfirst.[6] For more serious ills, however, she sometimes sent them to Lisa Žužek across the road, who had learned the healing arts from her father-in-law. Once Lisa treated Valentin's daughter Milka for a swollen and painful knee by laying a silk thread over it and making the sign of the cross several times. She told Milka to say three Hail Marys before going to bed and three on rising in the morning. When Milka arose in the morning her knee was already healed.

The care of their teeth was primitive. No one brushed his teeth, and no one went to a dentist. Lisa Žužek treated a child for toothache by praying over it and gesturing away from the child's jaw to induce the pain to leave. Once when Berta was crying with the pain of a toothache, her light-hearted aunt Neta tiptoed up behind her and poured a bucket of water over her head. This helped—for a while. Eventually most of the older people in Vižovlje lost all of their teeth. Neni Žužek, Franc's first cousin in the house diagonally across the road, used to yank out his own teeth with pliers when they became loose.

For serious illnesses little could be done. It cost too much to consult a doctor or to pay for an operation or for a stay of weeks or months in a hospital. The Žužeks and their neighbors had a kind of humble resignation to illness, and they also failed to realize what miracles medicine was beginning to work by the 1930s. Two doors away, the Klaričes were losing two children to tuberculosis, and the same would happen to the Žužeks' cousins with the same name across the road. Next door, Franc's sister Marija, as we noted earlier, was dying of the same disease; she is said to have been seen by a doctor only once.[7] The same disease, unresisted, was silently at work all over the Karst.

Franc's family was lucky to be spared from tuberculosis, but the illness and death of his baby daughter Nerina illustrates the relationship between want and death from disease. When the baby fell ill during her second year of life, no one knew what was wrong with her. (The parish priest would later record the cause of death simply as "weakness.") There could be no question of sending for a doctor, but Lojza could not cure her with the herbs she kept in a box in her bedroom, and neither could the older women in the hamlet whose advice she sought. The illness reached a crisis one September morning. Lojza sent for a neighbor, who urged her to treat the baby with juniper berries. While the neighbor was holding Nerina, Lojza started upstairs to fetch the berries. As she left the kitchen, she turned to look back at the baby, who turned her gaze on her mother. A few seconds later Nerina shuddered and died.

Yet despite the lack of doctors, the Žužeks and their neighbors were doing better now in the struggle with disease. In Vižovlje, as elsewhere, the life-threatening forces were still much in evidence, but the life-prolonging ones were gaining strength. There were still tubercular cows and tubercular people spreading their disease. There were still manure-strewn roads and flies. There were still lice and dirt. But on the other hand there was now somewhat better nutrition and therefore greater resistance to disease. There was abundant piped-in water. There was a midwife with a little medical training. There was a schoolteacher who taught hygiene and sent the children who had lice home to be deloused. And there was Franc Žužek, who was paid a very modest sum by the commune government to occasionally shovel up manure, which he used in his garden, from the roads in Vižovlje.

Whether one feels rich or poor depends very much on one's awareness of how others live, and within Vižovlje all lived on more or less the same level. But Franc's daughter Elda began to discover when she was about ten that some people were far richer than her family. On Sundays the Žužeks went sometimes to their parish church in Mavhinje and sometimes to a church near the sea in Sistiana that a younger brother of a count of Duino had built as his own chapel in the eighteenth century. In the 1930s his descendants lived during the summer in a villa near the chapel, and on Sundays they came to mass and sat in their own front-row pew. Others were welcome to attend the services. One Sunday the mother of the little Princess Diana noticed Elda and another girl of her age in the church and invited them to come and play with Diana. Elda went several times and on each occasion was astounded by some new revelation of wealth. Not only was Diana's house luxurious beyond anything she had seen, with rugs and curtains and paintings, but the little girl had her own child-sized playhouse. Here the children played with store-bought dolls, not the homemade Raggedy-Ann kind that were all that Elda had ever seen. Servants waited on them, bringing them hot chocolate and cookies. Most memorable of all, the chocolate was served in cups, each with its own saucer.

If the della Torre family served to remind the Žužeks that there were many who lived better than they, there were others to remind them of their own good fortune.[8] There were the bands of ragged gypsies who would suddenly appear in the hamlet telling fortunes and stealing whatever they could take, including, it was said, children. Housewives would scurry ahead of them to warn their friends to take down their laundry and shut their doors, and not to let the gypsy women hold their wedding rings while they told their fortunes. There was Švara, an old man who lived in a shack above the Žužeks' vegetable garden, who frequently begged for food. He promised one generous housewife that he would leave her the cache of coins he had hidden in a stone wall outside Vižovlje, but to her regret he died before he had revealed the hiding place. There was the wandering and ragged old woman to whom a housewife in Vižovlje gave an old dress. The woman changed into the dress by the side of the road to Slivno and left her ragged clothes by the roadside. Hundreds of lice boiled out of them, and a farmer who passed by and saw them called out his neighbors to see the astonishing sight. And there was Zorze from Lojza's hamlet, Cerovlje. He was a hulking, bullying beggar with a stick, who often appeared on the Žužek's doorstep at mealtime. During one winter in World War II he was found in a nearby field frozen to death.

Despite their hardships, the Žužeks' modest standard of living on the eve of World War II was clearly higher than that of their ancestors. They had more to eat, a more balanced diet, more and better clothing, and a somewhat more comfortable house. They also had the benefit of better roads, more water, access to a telephone for emergencies, a nearer and perhaps better school,[9] and more varied and interesting surroundings. Decades later Franc Žužek would look back over his life and conclude that life had been better, even during the Great Depression of the 1930s, than it had been when he was a little boy. In those earlier times the common lot was, he said, "misery." Compared to that low level, the Žužeks in the 1930s lived "like lords."

Now, however, they were to be thrown into the chaos and misery of a world war. Their improved standard of living would be in jeopardy. Simply to get through the war alive might be more than they could manage, even with all of the knowledge about how to survive in the face of adversity that they had absorbed from their ancestors on the Karst.

In June 1940 Italy entered World War II as Hitler's ally. For the next three years the impact of war on the little hamlet of Vižovlje, and on the lives of the Žužeks, was smaller than that of the Great War of 1914–18. Partisan bands formed and fought Mussolini's soldiers and police, but this time northeast Italy was not a war zone. No major battles were fought nearby, and the Žužeks were lucky to have no sons of fighting age. Food was not a grave problem, even when some hungry Italian soldiers at one point requisitioned the family's flock of chickens. Franc's garden provided vegetables and some fruit, and from time to time Lojza or Vida took the train to Ronchi, in the fertile Italian province of Friuli, and walked for miles from one isolated farmhouse to another buying small amounts of flour or cornmeal. The best currency for the purpose was the family's salt or cigarette ration.[10]

After the Allied invasion of southern Italy in 1943 and the collapse of Mussolini's government, however, the war turned grimmer for the people of the Karst. As Italy's German allies became her masters in the northern half of the peninsula and treated it like an occupied country, German troops replaced the Italian ones in Trieste and the Karst plateau above it. Vižovlje became a place of some concern to the Germans because the hamlet lay right alongside the railroad linking Trieste to northern Italy and offered a commanding view of the tracks leading to the west. German troops therefore commandeered a house in Vižovlje and made it into a general's headquarters.

In the meantime, young men from Vižovlje and the other hamlets in the Karst began slipping off into the woods in the interior to join the partisans. By the end of the war, ten men and boys from the fourteen families of Vižovlje had served with these ragged forces, and four of them had died.[11] From Nabrežina to Monfalcone small bands of these partisans would emerge from the woods at night to blow up the railroad tracks.[12] One of Vida Žužek's recollections gives a sense of the small scale and the daring of the partisan operations and the reason for a disaster that would soon strike the people of Vižovlje. One dark night a partisan band slipped out of the sparse woods above Vižovlje, entered the hamlet, and attacked the small German detachment. The Žužeks heard the first bullets and huddled at the back of their kitchen, as far as possible from the windows. Outside they heard much rifle fire and shouted commands in Slovene: "First company advance!" "Second company move to the right flank!" The Žužeks expected that with such large forces fighting they would wake up in the morning to find half the village destroyed. In fact, however, the physical damage proved to be slight. When Vida later asked a partisan friend about the battle, he laughingly told her that the attackers had numbered only seven.

From time to time the German occupiers would sweep through the hamlets in trucks and round up people of working age to send off to labor camps in Germany. One day when Vida was returning by train to Vižovlje from one of her foraging expeditions, she witnessed such a raid. German troops were lining up local men against the railroad fence, making them stretch their arms above their heads and press their foreheads against the wire. The soldiers were checking papers and shoving a few men into a truck. The passengers in the train, horrified and fearful, looked the other way. Fifteen men and women were carried off in this way from Vižovlje during the war; two of them died in German labor camps.[13]

In coping with the war, the Žužeks showed themselves to be as tricky as the gypsies, as stoic as the local beggars, and as skilled in survival arts as the country folk they were. Franc, always the adaptable laborer, found work with a company building air raid shelters in Monfalcone under German supervision. His job and his age—he was now in his mid-fifties—to some extent shielded him from the threat of the labor camps. Nevertheless the day came when German soldiers tried to take him away. Vida dashed into the house, found some medicines he was then taking for a minor illness, and showed them to the soldiers, who decided that he must be too infirm for the camps and let him go.

Franc's brother Valentin, next door, also escaped being carried off to do forced labor. A squad of German soldiers drove into the hamlet one day, parked near the station, and began rounding up men for the labor camps. Just before the soldiers arrived at his house, Valentin grabbed a walking stick, and when he followed the soldiers to the truck he was limping and leaning hard on his stick. He looked so pathetic that even his sister-in-law and nieces, who knew Valentin well, thought when they saw him that the roundup squad must have beaten him badly. When Valentin arrived at the station the German officer in charge observed Valentin's limp and his apparent decrepitude and told his men to release him because he would be no use as a laborer. As the truck and its load of captives pulled away Valentin threw away his stick and doubled over with laughter.

By 1944 Franc's son Angelo Žužek was sixteen and a likely candidate for forced labor. During one of the sudden German raids he was seized and carried off with a number of other men to a central deportation point at Gorizia. Angelo managed to slip out of the large crowd of prisoners and into a line of men destined to be sent to the labor camps. Then he sidled out of this and into another line of men who were to be given medical examinations. And finally he coolly slipped out of this one and into a line of men who had been examined and rejected. Finally the Germans told this group that they could go home, and Angelo quickly did so, walking across hills and fields to avoid being picked up again. Soon after he returned to Vižovlje, Franc and Lojza decided that Angelo would have to join the partisans in order to avoid forced labor or German military service. He left the village and served for several months with a ragged band of partisans. Occasionally he sneaked back into Vižovlje for a meal or a change of clothing, but in the evening he would return to the woods so that he would not be found at home after curfew. Eventually he returned home, somehow escaped the notice of the curfew patrols, and found a safe job in Monfalcone. *

How did the women of the Žužek family fare? Lojza continued to look after the house and family, coping as best she could with the worsening shortages. Berta became a live-in maid for a shopkeeper's family in Nabrežina. Elda, the youngest, saw her formal education come to an end when the local school closed. After that she helped her mother at home and embroidered napkins and towels for her hope chest, making them of old flour sacks and any other scraps of cloth she could find. On the occasions when the partisans blew up the railroad tracks near Vižovlje, she and other girls from the hamlet would meet the trains arriving at one end of the broken stretch of track and carry the bags of the passengers to the train waiting at the other end, earning a few lire.

Vida, now in her late teens, seems to have thrived under the challenges of the war. Increasingly it was she who took Franc's earnings and the family's cigarette rations to Friuli and walked from farm to farm, buying and trading for what cornmeal and other food she could find. And from time to time Vida carried food and letters from families in Vižovlje to partisan bands as far away as the Alpine foothills, trudging down lonely roads, though afraid of both the German patrols and the partisans. On one of these trips the leader of a guer-

---

* Clearly, for a sixteen year old, life with the partisans could be harsh. By contrast, for Angelo's twenty-year-old first cousin Franc Kočjančič, from nearby Cerovlje, serving with the partisans was the time of his life. He enjoyed the comradeship of his partisan band and wandered and fought with them all over the Karst and the Alpine foothills of Slovenia.

rilla band half urged her, half ordered her to join them. But Vida dreaded the danger, the hunger, and the squalor of their life. What may have been more important to a straight-laced Žužek, she was none too sure of the morals of the few women with the group. She told him that she considered his band no place for a woman, and he more or less conceded the point.[14]

By the summer of 1944 the attacks by the partisans were so effective that the Germans decided to destroy four of the hamlets that had helped to feed the guerrillas and provide them with information. Early in the morning of 16 August, an exceptionally hot day, truckloads of soldiers drove up to Vižovlje, Mavhinje, Cerovlje, and Medja vas. They encircled the little clusters of houses, and then soldiers rushed from one house to another shouting that in half an hour everything would be burned to the ground. In Vižovlje the Žužeks and their neighbors jumped from their beds and frantically considered what to do. Since it seemed likely that the soldiers would not only burn the houses but also carry many villagers off to labor camps, the family was uncertain whether to try to save their belongings or themselves.[15] Believing that Angelo might be deported, Franc and Lojza sent him off immediately to work. They and Vida and Elda then spent several minutes carrying out a few belongings. Then Franc, too, set off on foot to his job in Monfalcone. He was stopped once by a German soldier who looked at his identification card, hesitated, and then allowed him to proceed. Elda seized her winter coat and fled from the village, and Lojza and Vida soon followed, although they did not find Elda until hours later. From fields around the village they watched as the Germans set their fires, and the houses and stables were gutted by flames. Cows bellowed and pigs squealed in pain as the fires consumed them.

Within a couple of hours most of the houses, including those of Franc and Valentin, had been gutted by fire, and their tile roofs had crashed to the ground. Strangely enough, the fires set by the soldiers failed to catch in the three poorest homes in Vižovlje. The women who owned two of them decided that it would be better if their houses too should burn, since it seemed likely that some government would eventually pay the cost of rebuilding the village, and their houses could only be the better for rebuilding. They reentered the village and set fires in their own houses, but to no avail; for them as for the Germans, the houses would not take fire.

While Lojza and Vida were watching the village burn, a neighbor came up and told them that the German soldiers were rounding up the young women and that Vida had better report to them immediately to avoid being shot. When she turned herself in, Vida was taken to the courtyard of a house a mile from Vižovlje where numerous girls were under guard awaiting deportation.

Fig. 16. Fire-gutted houses of Franc Žužek (left) and Valentin Žužek (right), 1944. *Valentin's is the house (No. 2) where the Žužeks had lived since 1818. German troops burned Vižovlje and three other hamlets in 1944 in retaliation for railroad sabotage by local partisans. (Mervic-Legiša and Furlan, 1970.)*

An older woman who knew Vida happened along the road and saw her in the courtyard. Knowing some German, she approached the guard and somehow convinced him that Vida had had nothing to do with the partisans who had provoked the reprisals. At a time when his officer's attention was distracted, the guard surreptitiously signaled Vida to escape, and she did. She soon found Lojza, the two of them found Elda, and before long they went to a friend near Vižovlje and persuaded her to take in the family.[16]

A week or two later they moved to a little building between Vižovlje and Nabrežina that had formerly served as a Saturday night dance hall for quarry workers. It consisted simply of one large room and a large storage closet. Here they stayed until the end of the war, sleeping on the floor and sharing the use of a wood stove with another family who slept elsewhere. Meanwhile Franc took a new job away from home, helping to build a bomb shelter next to the German military hospital in Sežana.

At the beginning of this chapter we asked how the war would affect the lives and the living standard of a family that had only recently risen from want. To one who takes a long view of their history, one thing in particular stands out about their experience of World War II: the war did not merely check their progress; it threw them back into the historical past.

How far back? Considering the war's terror and destruction, we might say it picked up the Žužeks and hurled them clear back to the late Middle Ages. They found themselves once again in a society where the ruler was harsh and alien, where raiders torched whole villages, where armed men forced the populace to work for them, and where old enemies settled their scores at night and left the bodies by the roadside.

But looked at from another point of view—its impact on their economic life—the war carried the Žužeks back not to the late Middle Ages but to the mid-nineteenth century. It set them down in those decades when industrialization had just begun to affect their lives. True, the resemblance is not perfect. Franc Žužek did not begin to till the soil with oxen or tend a flock of sheep. But consider the many similarities. Once again the Žužeks lived in the same cramped conditions that their ancestors had known when they lived on one side of a two-story house, sharing the first floor with their cattle and the second floor with the hayloft. Once again they had almost no clothes but those on their backs. Once again food was not merely limited in kind but actually scarce, and there were times when they went to bed hungry. Some of the services provided by the government vanished as well. The village school closed. Roads deteriorated. The railroad functioned, but only when the partisans had not recently blown up a stretch of the tracks.

But if it was worse than uncomfortable to be thrown back into the nineteenth century, the Žužeks could probably adjust more easily than many others, especially those in the cities. In their large garden they could at least grow some food of their own, and they could buy a little more from their farm friends nearby or from other farmers a few miles away in Friuli. Other country people in Europe's war-torn lands probably had a little more to eat than many who lived in the cities. So it was with the Žužeks. It seems likely that they also adjusted to some of the hardships of war better than the more comfortably off—whether in town or country—who went through the same experience. For the Žužeks, getting by without a doctor was nothing new. It was no hardship not to be able to drive a car when they had never owned one, or to find train travel restricted when they were already used to walking great distances to save train fares. It was no sacrifice to trade their cigarette rations for food when smoking was a luxury they had never been able to afford. For Franc and Lojza, if not so much for their children, many wartime hardships were no worse than the "misery," to repeat Franc's term, that they had known as children.

What also made it easier for them than for others to adjust to the return to a preindustrial economy was that Franc and Lojza could use the preindustrial skills that they had learned growing up in Vižovlje and Cerovlje at the turn of the century. Franc carved a wooden spindle, and when Lojza managed to get some sheep's wool she spun it into thread and then knitted stockings for her family. She stitched coils of rags together to make the primitive sandals that she had worn years earlier as a milkmaid. When the Žužeks bought dried corn from farmers, Franc fashioned a primitive mortar and pestle and ground the kernels into meal. And when Lojza could beg or save some animal fat, she percolated water through wood ashes to leech out the lye and mixed it with the fat to make soap. Like other families only a generation or two removed from preindustrial life, the Žužeks were well equipped not only to endure the privations of war but to cope actively with a suddenly primitivized economy. Perhaps this has been the experience of many such families struggling to survive in wartime social disintegration.

The terror and privations finally came to an end. In April 1945, while partisan armies closed in on Trieste from other directions, the British Eighth Army swept northeast toward the city along Italy's Adriatic coast. On May 1 the Second New Zealand Division captured Monfalcone, the ship-building town where Franc had worked from time to time. At 8:30 on the morning of May 2 the New Zealand forces set out for Trieste along the old road built by the Romans two millennia ago. When they reached Duino and Sistiana, not far from the gutted and smoke-blackened houses of Vižovlje, they captured some Germans who were guarding gun positions. The New Zealanders pointed their tanks toward the sea and fired on three German vessels, setting one on fire and forcing the crew to abandon another.[17]

At this point the road to Trieste forks, so the New Zealanders divided their forces in two. One force headed straight for Trieste down the coastal road that Franc, years before, had helped to carve out of the cliffs. The other followed the old Roman road, which proceeds through the Karst for several miles before dropping down to Trieste. Along the road just in front of them were German troops, retreating from the New Zealanders and trying at the same time to cope with harassing fire from Slovene partisans.

On this stretch of road, more or less in open country, was the Žužeks' little dance-hall house. As it happened, Franc was a short distance away. The others at home could hear the rifles and artillery fire of the Germans and partisans and the approaching New Zealanders. A German soldier running past the house saw Angelo inside the doorway. He dashed in, shouted "Partisan!" and pointed his rifle at the eighteen-year-old boy. Berta threw herself between them. No, she tried to explain, this is not a partisan, he is my brother and he works digging bomb shelters. Meanwhile she shouted over her shoulder to Angelo to show his identity card. Just then there was a burst of rifle fire from somewhere near the house. The soldier ran off, and the Žužeks jumped into the shelter they had dug in the floor of the large all-purpose room. They could hear fierce fighting on all sides. Then, suddenly, it stopped. Franc, who had just seen the approaching New Zealand troops, ran into the house, shouting, "The war is over!" Then he ran out and shouted in the direction of the woods across the road, "Come out! It's over! The war is over!" Out of the woods walked a dozen ragged, dirty, bearded partisans. They and the Žužeks all fell on each other's necks, laughing and weeping. The terror and hardships of war were over. The Žužeks could resume their rise from want.

10

Tarnished Miracle

In the Karst, as elsewhere in much of the industrialized or industrializing world, the years immediately after World War II were hard ones, but by the late 1940s improvement was visible. The industrialized nations, Italy included, had begun a dramatic recovery.[1] In the early 1950s Italy's boom turned into the "Italian miracle." United States Marshall Plan aid provided much of the capital, but Italian investors themselves felt new confidence and helped to pay for the rebuilding. The government stabilized the lira. Energy from oil and gas was still cheap. Italian cars, typewriters, shoes, dresses, and other products sold well at home and abroad. By 1951 Italy's industrial production was almost half again what it had been on the eve of World War II, and it continued to rise rapidly until the early 1960s.[2]

Even the Karst shared in the "Italian miracle." (When we speak of the Karst in this chapter we mean the western part of it, the Žužeks' homeland; the eastern part was awarded to Yugoslavia after World War II.) Across its rocky fields and pastures the Italian government built the northeasternmost extension of its new system of superhighways. Meanwhile, as Trieste prospered,[3] her people were building villas on the Karst, thus pouring money into the pockets of the farmers who sold them their rocky pastures and also providing work for home builders. The quarries thrived as European governments and their prospering middle classes sought fine limestone and marble for their post offices, train stations, stadiums, office buildings, and high-rises.[4] Perhaps the greatest new force in the local economy was a huge paper mill, the Cartiera del Timavo, which a Swiss-Italian firm built on the coast between Duino and Monfalcone. By the late 1970s it employed nearly a thousand men and women. From Karst villages and from towns in Friuli they came by car and train for one of three shifts, earning good wages in return for hard and monotonous work, and for putting up with terrific noise and a work discipline that they had never known before.[5]

As time passed during these booming postwar decades, other kinds of jobs became more common. Children of farmers and quarrymen opened grocery stores to serve the new suburbanites. Others found work in hotels and restaurants that catered to tourists on their way to the Dalmatian coast in Yugoslavia. Thus a service sector developed alongside the ancient farming sector and the much newer industrial one.[6]

The Žužeks had never known what it was to have ample food, medical care, and economic security. Life on the Karst had changed profoundly. We shall be exploring here how they adjusted to this age of greater plenty.

By the end of 1946 Vižovlje and the three other burned-out hamlets had been rebuilt with German reparations money. The Žužeks packed up their scanty belongings and lugged them across the fields and back to their old home. The rebuilt house looked pretty much as it had before the war. Franc found second-hand furniture to replace most of what had been burned. He hauled away the rubble of war that covered much of his garden and began growing vegetables again, and before long he had also planted apricots and figs, trained grapes over arbors in the courtyard and behind the house, and started another flock of chickens. Most important, he again found a job as a laborer in a shipyard at Monfalcone. It was here that he had held one of his earliest jobs, four decades earlier, and admired the competent young British engineers and experimented disastrously with smoking a pipe.

In the early 1950s, as the "Italian miracle" took place, the Žužeks began to live better than they ever had before. Unionization was helping Franc to profit from the economic boom. In all his previous working life Franc had never held a unionized job, and therefore he had been paid as little as his employer could get away with. As we have shown, on one occasion in the 1920s, when he complained that his pay as a quarry laborer was low, his boss answered, "Would nothing be better?" His pay as a shipyard laborer just before World War II, he used to say, had been "a black and a white" (which means "peanuts"). But in postwar Italy unions were legal, and Franc's shipyard pay rose significantly as a strong union negotiated for the workers.

At the same time Franc's two children who remained at home were in their twenties, and they began to earn enough at least to pay for their clothes and incidental expenses. Franc could now electrify his house and pipe water into his kitchen.[7] The Žužeks' medical care improved when a doctor settled in nearby Sistiana and Italy's socialized medicine began to pay for his services. There was a growing economic security in the Žužeks' lives, for the postwar Italian government dramatically extended the number of people covered by its obligatory social insurance schemes and sharply raised the payments.[8] When Franc retired in 1954 and Lojza fell victim to crippling arthritis, they received monthly payments that covered their small expenses.

Around them the Žužeks could see a rapid transformation of the little hamlet they knew so well. With the new prosperity there were changes in the look, the sounds, and even the smell of Vižovlje. Television aerials sprouted above the red tile roofs. A few Vespas, light motorcycles, showed up on the dusty roads, and after a while a few small cars. Then the dust vanished when the communal government paved the roads. As the farmers grew old and their children abandoned farming, fewer cows clomped through the hamlet on the new asphalt, and the roar of Vespas was heard more often than the squealing of pigs. Flies vanished, and so did the pungent smell of manure.[9]

Suburbanization began. First a young Slovene housepainter and his wife,

Fig. 17. Marija Colja, midwife, taking cows to pasture. *From about 1900 until 1951 she was the midwife of Vižovlje. (Courtesy of* Primorski Dnevnik, Trieste.)

who had rented two rooms from a neighbor of the Žužeks, built themselves a house fifty yards beyond the edge of the hamlet. Lojza marveled that anyone would want to live outside the warm, compact little settlement, "among the vipers." Before long, however, prosperous businessmen from Trieste began buying fields from Valentin Žužek and other farmers and building themselves villas on all sides of the hamlet. (The stones of the prehistoric fortification on the hill above Vižovlje were hauled away to make room for a garden.) Within a couple of decades Vižovlje took on the shape of a ring and a core. In the ring were the villas with green lawns and handsome flower gardens planted on dirt trucked in to cover the Karst's rocky crust. In the core were the fourteen old houses and their barns, some of them newly plastered and painted, but shabby in the company of their new neighbors. Living in the ring were the well-dressed suburbanites who spoke Italian, the language of commerce and government, and drove to the city each day in Volkswagens and Alfa Romeos.[10] In the old houses of the core were the old Slovene population, the Žužeks and their neighbors, living better than their ancestors but less well than the growing suburbanite population around them. Their Slovene language, which had always marked them as members of an under class when they went out of Vižovlje, now identified them as a minority even in their own hamlet, strangers in their own land.

In the difficult postwar years and then in the prosperous years that followed, it was the four Žužek children, not their parents, who had to seize opportunities and make choices. Angelo, the only son, at first found it hard to find a job to his liking, and the problem of their son's employment troubled his parents for several years. As the son of a shipyard worker, Angelo was entitled to special consideration if he applied for work in the same yard. Such jobs were particularly desirable in the difficult postwar years because they paid well and there were few layoffs. To his family's dismay, however, Angelo spurned the opportunity and chose an inferior job as an apprentice welder in Trieste.

The steps taken by his mother in this crisis show how seriously the family took the matter of helping their son to find the right work. Consulting with friends, Lojza learned that the priest of the Greek-Illyrian church in Trieste could be especially helpful in such matters. If she would bring an item of Angelo's clothing and speak to no one en route to the church, the priest would pray over the garment for Angelo's enlightenment. Lojza decided that rather than take the train, on which she might meet friends who would speak to her, she would walk the eleven miles to Trieste. While she was walking by the side of the main road to the city, a friend passed in a truck, saw her, and stopped to offer a ride. He called to her but was dumbfounded as Lojza turned away without answering and struck out across country. She reached Trieste and spoke to the priest, who offered up the necessary prayers. Some time later his prayers appeared to bear fruit when Angelo took a job in Monfalcone as a shipyard welder.

The changing forms of transportation that Angelo used to get to school and work provide a good index of the Karst's slowly rising prosperity. As a boy he had walked or ridden his father's bicycle. After World War II he used the train to go to work until, in about 1950, he was able to afford a Vespa. By about 1960 he was driving a second-hand Fiat 500, a tiny car powered so low that on the superhighway he had to hug the right-hand lane. By 1972 he had purchased a second-hand but still magnificent Citroën, a vehicle that roared down the superhighway and could, at the touch of a button, raise or lower itself several inches with respect to its axles.

Franc's three daughters—Berta, Vida, and Elda—also chose their paths in the decade after the war. They seem to have been partly influenced by the general inclination of young women of the Karst to leave their hamlets and to seek jobs and husbands nearer the cities. Perhaps such girls first caught a glimpse of the more leisurely, more comfortable urban life when their boyfriends took them on their Vespas to dance in the seaside cafés that were also frequented by prosperous Triestines. Meanwhile, movies and then television acquainted them with an urban lifestyle—usually an American one—wildly different from what they had known on the Karst. At the same time the "Italian miracle" was producing the jobs that made it possible for them to begin to realize their dreams. Thus they sought and found work in the larger hamlets and villages, and even in Monfalcone and Trieste, as maids, barmaids, factory workers, and even sales clerks. (As late as the 1940s, young women from nearby hamlets who worked in Trieste walked to Vižovlje to take the train. They left home wearing old shoes for the walk over the rough country roads and carrying their good city shoes in bags. Just before they reached Vižovlje they put on the good shoes and hid the old ones in holes in the stone walls by the roadside, where they could often be spotted by passers-by.) During this period such women began to marry up, choosing husbands from hamlets bigger than their own—or better still, men from places like Vižovlje, with easy access to the cities—or, best of all, men from the cities themselves.

Berta, a tall and striking blonde, was particularly anxious to leave Vižovlje. Having had very little schooling, she could usually find work only as a maid, and she moved from her wartime job in Nabrežina to others in Trieste.

Later, guided by her wanderlust and suggestions from friends who had worked abroad, she moved to other jobs in Venice, Switzerland, and finally in London. Along the way she had numerous suitors but none who suited her. Finally, while she was working in a hospital in London, she met and married an East Indian who worked both in a government office and as a telephone operator. They bought themselves a flat in a London suburb.

Vida, the Žužeks' second daughter, suffered from a congenital eye disorder. She could see only poorly, and her prospects must have seemed very uncertain. She was also tenacious and intelligent, however, as she had shown when she foraged for her family's food during the war. After much searching she found secure part-time work in a semi-state-owned food market. This virtually guaranteed her a steady income, but a very low one. She would always, it seemed, depend on her parents or her brother to provide a home.

In the early 1950s, however, she resolved this problem too. Some years earlier she had begun to bet a small sum each week in the Italian national soccer lottery. To win, one had to predict correctly the winners, or the ties, in thirteen national soccer league games played on a given Sunday. By this time the Italian economic boom was under way, and each week millions of people purchased lottery tickets, so that the possible winnings were large. Vida's method of predicting outcomes was hardly scientific. She cared nothing about soccer and knew nothing about the different teams. As she filled out her lottery card, she predicted the outcomes by spinning with her fingers a small wooden top, with markings around its middle, and writing down whatever marking (1, 2, or X, for team number one, team number 2, or a tie) faced up when the top stopped spinning and fell on a side. Finally one week Vida was among the winners. She received 2.7 million lire, or about forty-three hundred dollars. This was a very large sum by the standards of the Karst at the time, and far larger than any Žužek had ever seen.

Friends suggested various ways to spend the money, including a trip around the globe. Vida thought about it, and instead of circling the globe she walked across the road to the house of a retired farmer in Vižovlje. From him she bought a third of an acre of land in a large field below Vižovlje traditionally called "Brajda" (which means plowed field), and here she built a comfortable little house. Since she would never marry and her earnings could never be large, the winning of the lottery had been a great stroke of good fortune. Sheer luck and optimism had allowed her to tap the new industrial prosperity and assure her future well-being.

Elda, the youngest Žužek daughter, loved the life of her hamlet with its familiar ways and faces, but she was drawn at the same time to the city. Trieste offered store windows full of elegant clothes and needlework, crowds of strikingly dressed and exuberant Triestines, outdoor cafés on sunny piazzas. Above all it offered what was so dear to a modern Žužek, the possibility of clean indoor work. She found a job in the city as a seamstress's helper, pulling threads from hems, basting, running errands, and gradually learning the trade. The pay was very poor, however, so she later found work helping to run an American army snack bar.[*] Here in 1954 she met a lanky, bespectacled American soldier who wrote for the local army newspaper, and the two became engaged. When she brought him home to meet her family, Franc told the American that the family liked him well enough but did not want Elda to go so far away. Nonetheless Franc made no strong objection. The two were married and soon left for the United States, where Elda's husband became a historian and the writer of this book.

Berta's and Elda's choices of spouses contrast sharply with all of the known previous marriages in their family. Their ancestors had almost always chosen men and women from hamlets within walking distance of their own, which in effect means that they chose their spouses from within a group of about one hundred fifty families. Just how small the range of choice was is shown by the fact that their great-great-grandfather Matija had married a woman named Lupinc from Praprot, and their uncle Valentin, a century later, had married a woman with the same surname from the same tiny hamlet. Their grandfather Jožef[II] had married a Caharija from Nabrežina, and seventy-five years later their first cousin Stanko had also married a Caharija from Nabrežina. Their great-grandfather Jožef[I] and their first cousin Milka had both married second cousins, and other Žužeks had probably done the same. Now, working not as farm girls on the Karst but in towns, and living in a world with an increasingly mobile population, Berta and Elda had married men from the Asian subcontinent and North America.

In the late 1950s this story of a family's rise from want nears its end. Franc and his wife and children had seen and enjoyed the triumph of industrialization. Franc had retired with a small pension and in a modest comfort that far outshone anything his forefathers had known. Angelo now worked at a steady job that was more highly skilled and better paid than any job that a Žužek had ever held. Berta and Elda had ventured into urban job markets and emerged

---

[*] American and British forces were garrisoned in Trieste from 1945 to 1954, when Italy and Yugoslavia finally reached an agreement about their border south of Trieste.

as middle-class housewives in distant countries. Vida had found work that met the family's highest requirements—light and clean and performed indoors—and by a stroke of luck had tapped for herself an ample share of the great pool of new wealth produced by an industrial economy.

The relative prosperity of these last decades of Franc's life could not shield him from the problems of old age. He remained healthy, but Lojza was increasingly crippled with arthritis. Her family blamed this on her years of hard work, and particularly on the period when she not only looked after her own house but also helped her widowed sister with her farm work in a distant hamlet. In addition to arthritis, Lojza suffered from diabetes and glaucoma. During the last quarter of her life, Franc, with help from Vida, spent much of his time caring for her.

Meanwhile there were also problems with Angelo and his wife. When Angelo was in his early thirties, he married Danila, a woman from Praprot who, like him, had fought with the local partisans in the war. Since Angelo was not yet earning enough to buy a house of his own, he and Danila were forced to live with his parents. In the Karst the oldest son and his wife, as we have seen, had traditionally lived with his parents and looked after them in their old age,[*] but times had changed. With government pensions and medical care, the elderly could often manage financially without their children's help. Since almost nobody was farming, the labor of young people was no longer needed at home. At the same time, newly married couples were more likely to find now that they could afford to buy or rent a place of their own. Thus it was no longer the invariable rule for young couples to live with and help their parents. Angelo and Danila, however, were obliged by need to live under the same roof, and they felt crowded, put upon, and frustrated. They adopted a baby boy, but it was hard to raise him amid so many family strains.

Lojza died in 1976 at the age of eighty. Berta flew from London to the funeral. As soon as it was over, she and Vida packed up their father's clothes, and Franc, now eighty-eight years old, moved to Vida's small house just below Vižovlje. Here he would live for the last two years of his life, looking after a small vegetable garden and passing the hours when Vida was away at work as best he could. Franc was the first Žužek in the line of descent we have followed in this book not to remain under the same roof with his or her oldest

---

[*] In the early 1800s Jernej Gabrovic and his wife lived with their oldest daughter (they had no living son) and her husband, Tomaž Žužek, until their deaths. Tomaž in turn lived with his son and daughter-in-law until his death. Later in the same century Jožef[I] and his wife lived with Jožef[II] and Marija until their deaths.

son until death. A combination of personality clashes and the new prosperity had caused a break with ancient custom. [11]

Angelo and Danila remained in the old house in Vižovlje, but Franc eventually decided to sell the house and divide the proceeds among his four children. Angelo protested, claiming that as the only son, and one with a child to raise, his claim to and need for his father's legacy was greater than his sisters'. Certainly it was true that for generations the Žužeks and other Karst families had left their houses to their oldest sons, but Franc held firm. Eventually he fixed a price for the house and sold it to Angelo, allowing him to deduct his own quarter-share from the price he paid. Franc never explained his reasons for dividing his property evenly among his children, beyond saying that it was "fair." [12] Perhaps in the back of his mind he had nourished for two-thirds of a century some sense of injustice that his father's property had gone entirely to his older brother, only to be taken over later by the detested Valentin.

Often in these last years of his life Franc would walk from his daughter's house to a rocky bluff some fifty yards below it. Here he liked to look down on the superhighway that stretched like an ugly scar across the land where his forefathers had watched their sheep and tended their vines. Now on the superhighway the cars and trucks hurtled past him, horns blaring, tires screaming as they passed with a rising and falling pitch, the wind in their wake blowing against him. He could see trailer trucks bringing steers fattened in Yugoslavia to slaughterhouses in Italy, other behemoths bearing fruit from Greece and Rumania to the northwestern corner of Europe, shiny Italian cars taking the new suburbanites of the Karst to their work in Trieste, husky flatbed trucks hauling slabs of polished local marble to building sites in northern Italy, and powerful German cars whisking Austrian tourists to the beaches of the Dalmatian coast.

The sight of such a change could hardly fail to stir Franc, as he stood there, to reflect on the past of the Karst and of himself. Of course, there was much of that past that even he, as he reached the age of ninety, knew nothing about. Because of his parents' ignorance and the scantiness of his own schooling, he had no idea that the rocks he stood on had once been under the sea, nor that prehistoric hunters had once prowled this land, nor that his own Slovene ancestors had settled here over a millennium ago, nor that ancestors of the prince at Duino had formerly owned all of this land and Franc's ancestors as well (though in a way he sensed this). While he greatly admired "the old ones" who had painstakingly cleared the local fields and built the thick stone walls around them, he knew almost nothing about them.

Fig. 18. Franc Žužek at eighty-five.

But if he knew very little about the broader and deeper past, he had personally witnessed a great deal and had reflected upon it. Thanks, as he would say, to having always "worked hard" and eaten home-grown food, he had lived nine full decades.* He had experienced World War I, the end of the Austro-Hungarian Empire, fascism, and World War II, but above all he had lived

---

* Karst people who, like Franc, survived childhood illnesses and many privations often survived long past three score years and ten. Antonija Gabrovic of Vižovlje trotted out to the pasture and back twice daily with her cows until, when she was ninety-seven, an Allied bombing attack in World War II literally frightened her to death. Lisa Žužek, whose folk remedies were mentioned earlier, walked daily to Mavhinje to attend mass until one day, in her ninety-sixth year, she was crossing the railroad tracks and failed to hear an approaching express.

through the process of industrialization almost from its start. In his boyhood most of the people of the Karst had been little more than subsistence farmers living in what he described as "misery." He had himself driven a great steam-roller to flatten the gravel for the roads, poured water and sand under the wire that cut the stone for the buildings, and hauled the lumber and steel for the ships that transformed the old preindustrial world.

Franc viewed most of the changes in life on the Karst, and especially the dramatic ones since World War II, with the same interest and enthusiasm with which he watched traffic on the superhighway.[13] In many ways life was better. Everybody had more to eat, especially the children, who now grew so tall that they towered over him.[14] No longer did you see hungry, lice-ridden old people walking the country roads and begging. Nowadays almost no one had tuberculosis. If you were sick, you could see a doctor at no cost. If you needed teeth, you could buy them, as Valentin had done. People dressed far better. Young village women dressed like sales clerks in dress shops—and sometimes they really were sales clerks in dress shops.

No longer did you have to walk everywhere or sit on a cart watching the rear end of a plodding ox. Most families had cars now and rode everywhere in a flash, as Angelo did in his self-lifting Citroën. He could remember an old couple in Vižovlje during World War I who saw an observation plane in the sky above them and, astonished, guessed from its shape that it was a giant hay rake. Now old women who had spent most of their lives leading cows to pasture, switch in hand, got into planes and jetted off to see Red Square or the Egyptian pyramids. Berta flew down from London from time to time, and Elda and her family flew back from America.

With all of the new machinery, work was ridiculously easy. In his time Franc had chopped post holes out of solid rock, loaded stone in carts, hauled timbers, shoveled up the manure of cart horses, and spaded great piles of sand and cement to make concrete. Now people came home from their jobs looking as if they had scarcely moved a muscle, and yet their pay was so good that they put in bathrooms, ripped out the stone floors in the kitchens and replaced them with marble tiles, and remodeled their old barns as extra living quarters. The ones who could sell old scraps of pasture to wealthy Triestines, like Valentin, had more money than they knew what to do with. Most of them abandoned their old houses in Vižovlje and built new ones on the edge of the hamlet, next to the elegant villas of the Triestines. And now there was luxury even in the grave. Once you were lucky if they put a simple wooden cross above you with your name scrawled on the crosspiece. Now the dead lay under handsome slabs of polished marble or granite topped with their photo-graphs reproduced in ceramic tiles.

And yet, Franc believed, in some ways the new prosperity had made things worse. The new villas were elegant, and the highway offered him something to look at, but on the whole the Karst was uglier. The superhigh-way was no thing of beauty. Where they had laid an underground oil pipe, which ran from Trieste to Germany and Austria, there was a scar of churned-up rock miles long where no junipers or blackberries would grow for a very long time. The paper factory was an ugly blight on the coastline beyond the Timavo. Pretty pastures had been ripped up to make sites for houses. In many places, trash and building rubble had been dumped by the roadside.

The things that used to give shape to life seemed to be falling apart. Reli-gion meant little or nothing to most people. Only the old people and some women and small children still went to mass on Sundays at the little churches in Sistiana and Mavhinje. Family relationships seemed to be deteriorating. Old people were confused by all the changes, and their children and grand-children had no need for their advice. Married couples did not want their old parents around any more and wouldn't look after them. Husbands and wives quarreled a lot. You could hear them as you walked through a hamlet. And parents let their children get away with too much. Once they had been too harsh, but now they had gone the other way.

It wasn't just husbands and wives who quarreled. Everybody did, much more than they used to. Workmen quarreled at their jobs, neighbors quarreled over their walls, children quarreled coming home from school. Vižovlje, which used to be like a large family, had lost its unity. The children didn't play those far-ranging games of hide-and-seek. The older people no longer played bocce or gathered after supper to chat in the little square above the train tracks.[15] Neighbors didn't help each other the way they used to, even down to the end of the second war. But then, nobody needed help the way they used to.

It was all right to think about all of these things, but there was no point trying to tell others about them. They didn't want to be told that life was once much harder. That was boring and depressing, and anyway they were sure that if life used to be harder, it was because people used to be stupider. As for telling them that in some ways the quality of life had declined, it was better to forget that. Life looked pretty good to them. They didn't want to hear some oldster who didn't understand what was going on telling them what was wrong with their world.[16]

Those were the kinds of thoughts Franc had as he watched the traffic on the superhighway. Eventually he would turn around and go back to Vida's house to pass the time as best he could until her return.

One day in November of 1978, while Vida was at work, Franc suffered a stroke. He died a week later and was buried in the cemetery of Sistiana in a plot next to Lojza's and adjacent to one that was waiting for Valentin. Over Franc and Lojza's grave is a slab of imported black granite, its perfect polish suggestive of the new prosperity.

A Suggestion About the Larger Picture

This was the story of ordinary people doing simple things: Jurij Žužek paying his lord his dues; a woman walking through a famine-struck countryside seeking food for her family and coming home empty-handed; Tomaž witnessing the deaths of most of his children before his own burial in "the black earth"; Marijana, at forty-two, giving birth to her twelfth child after her husband's death from "putrid fever"; Jožef[I] hauling water to the builders of a new railroad; Ivan Baptist masquerading as a rich man; the cousins, Franc and Ivan, brawling in a tavern in Trieste; Karlina feeling her heart leap into her mouth as she first laid eyes on her future husband; Jožef[II] arriving home sprawled dead on his ox cart; Valentin, a youngest son, taking over the family house and lands; the tubercular Marija being beaten by her brother; Emil drinking himself to sleep while on duty as a watchman; Lojza falling sick of typhus in the Great War; Franc meekly asking his boss for a raise; Berta, hungry, nibbling her father's lunch as she carried it to the quarry; Vida winning a lottery and building a house.

One contribution of this history has been simply to retell the story of these poor peasants and laborers. Such people once made up most of the populace even in the industrializing areas of the globe, but historians have been able to write about them mainly as statistical abstractions. There is something to be said for having re-evoked as vividly as the sources allowed the lives of some very ordinary flesh-and-blood individuals who ruled no lands, ran no wars, owned no ships, saved no souls, and penned no poems, but who helped to make life possible for those who did.

But this book has done more than simply to put flesh on such abstractions as *peasant* and *laborer*. It has also contributed to our understanding of some widespread social changes. Most of the Žužeks who appear in this book probably believed that they lived outside of what they imagined to be history. In fact, however, they experienced many of the great changes that the industrialized world was undergoing. These changes included among others the end of the mastery of the landowners, the growth of a world economy, a decline in death rates and then a decline in birth rates, industrialization, the spread of literacy, the shaping of a more democratic kind of family, total war, suburbanization, and a remarkable rise in living standards.

With the example of one family one cannot prove anything, but I finish the writing of this family history feeling that many millions of poor families who left almost no traces of their existence must have experienced these broad changes in something like the way the Žužeks did. In other rural economies like that of the Karst the abundance of land or the lack of it (before our period of change) may well have determined whether a peasant family would either swiftly multiply or cautiously limit its numbers so as simply to survive in its tiny niche. One might guess that with other illiterate peasants, as with the Žužeks, their recollection of their earlier life as serfs was very dim and their understanding of the way that life ended—a profound change in their being—was very confused. It seems likely that the decline of infant mortality among peasants elsewhere, as with the Žužeks, occurred as a result of numerous small improvements in their living conditions. Industrialization probably began to affect the lives of many peasants, as it did those of the Žužeks, long before it developed into anything like an industrial revolution.

And so with a number of this book's other findings. The experiences of the Žužeks must have been something like the experiences of many millions of other peasant and laboring families of the Machine Age, nearly traceless ones, who also rose from want.

Notes

Preface

1. At the time, most of the thirteen hundred households in the Triestine Karst owned from two and a half to seven and a half acres (one to three hectares) of land. Of the thirteen hundred heads of household, about two hundred were full-time farmers. The others were town workers and part-time farmers (Arnez 1958: 177; Caharija 1975–76: 64).

2. Little has been written about the social and economic history of the Triestine Karst. Cannarella (1968 and 1975) provides a survey from prehistory to modern times. Moritsch (1969) offers detailed economic histories of eight hamlets and a useful bibliography. Semerani, de Rosa, and Celli (1970) includes Diana de Rosa's historical sketch of a Karst fishing village, and Bratuž et al. (1983) contains essays on the history of Duino. The large histories by Grafenauer (1954–78) and Čepič et al. (1979) deal with Yugoslavian Slovenia and scarcely mention the Triestine Karst.

Chapter 1: Serfs' Niches

1. Obviously I am simplifying the possible consequences of a relative shortage of land. Where land was scarce, people could sometimes turn from low-yield crops such as wheat to high-yield crops such as potatoes, if these were available; they could farm marginal land, if they had it; they could emigrate, if this was feasible. In many places, moreover, wars and epidemics limited the population sufficiently so that the availability of land was not a factor in living standards and population change.

2. Malthus 1798: chap. 7. A number of contemporaries of Malthus in Europe, China, Japan, and probably elsewhere made much the same point (Spengler 1942; Silberman 1959–60; Overbeek 1970; Keene 1952: 257–65; Hutchinson 1967: 110–39).

3. Le Roy Ladurie (1974) tells a rather complex story in which not only the

availability of land but also war, taxes, disease, and technology are major variables. Among the countless other works that touch on land and population change, see Lucas (1930); Genicot (1966: 661–77); Goubert (1960: chaps. 2, 4, 5, 8); Edwards and Williams (1956); Helleiner (1967: 75–77); Katz (1972: 113, 322); and Easterlin (1976a and 1976b). Collomp (1983) shows how families in a French village with a fixed number of houses and limited farmland adapted by using a stem family system, stern patriarchy, primogeniture, and so on, adapting to their tight niche much as we shall suggest that the Žužeks did to theirs.

4. On karstic formations in general see Herak and Stringfield (1972) and Sweeting (1973).

5. Cannarella 1975: 11–15.

6. Ibid., 113–29, 155–61; Cannarella 1980. The road was the southern branch of the Via Gemina.

7. Čermelj (Kos et al. 1974: 5) says that the Slovenes settled in the Triestine Karst in the sixth century. Cannarella (1975: 176–79) seems to suggest they settled there in about the year 1000, give or take a century or two. There is almost no documentary or archeological evidence bearing on the point.

8. Regarding the deforestation, see Pichler (1882: 75) and Cannarella (1975: 50–51, 178).

9. Even in the sixteenth century this road was so rough that it took six oxen to pull a cart along it.

10. Cusin 1937: vol. 1, 80–88. Actually Rudolf died a year before Ugo of Duino agreed to render homage, but Rudolf had made Ugo's submission inevitable.

11. Were the Duino peasants in fact serfs? I think so. The Duino charter of 1578 makes clear that they farmed land that belonged to their lord and paid for its use with labor services, guard duty, firewood, food, and money (Archivio di Stato di Trieste [henceforth AST], Atti amm. di Gorizia, 1754–83, container 48, folder 493, "Urbar Herrschafft Tibein"). Although the lord owned the land, the head of each serf family had the right to bequeath the use of the land to a son. It is not clear whether the serfs might leave the land, but given the lack of opportunity for them elsewhere, why would they have chosen to do so? The lord may sometimes have told them whom to marry (Pichler 1882: 152–53), and his court administered justice to them. The lord may even have had the "right of the first night" with his serfs' brides, although this is certainly not mentioned in the charter. A local tradition says that he did (see Chapter 3).

12. Pichler 1882: 147, 273, 366–88, 407. In 1587 the della Torre family, wealthy Italian nobles, became lords of Duino and vassals of the Hapsburgs. Their descendants occupy the castle to this day.

13. For a useful survey of this trend, see Slicher van Bath (1967: 113–23).

14. There may have been another, closely related reason for issuing a new charter. Five years earlier there had been a great peasant rebellion in Croatia and parts of Carniola. It is said to have sparked peasant unrest over an even wider area, possibly including Duino, although there was no actual uprising there (Adamček 1968). After its suppression the Hapsburgs tried to correct some of the abuses that had led to the revolt (Guldescu 1970: 85). No doubt one reason for satisfying peasant grievances was the same need for a united front against the Turks that caused Charles to unite his lands into a single military unit. In any case, the serf rebellion of 1573 may have played a role in leading Charles to issue a new charter.

15. AST, "Urbar Herrschafft Tibein."

16. The Žužeks are not mentioned in a Duino charter of 1494 (Kos 1939–54: vol. 3, 206–22).

17. Doria 1971: 228.

18. They would have used this water for drinking and cooking and a discreet amount of washing. Cattle were watered in a village pond, which trapped rainwater.

19. On the architectural history of the Karst farmhouse, see Nice (1940) and M. P. Pagnini (1966).

20. For a description of typical manorial dues in Croatia and parts of Slovenia in the sixteenth century, see Adamček (1968: 44).

21. Two centuries later his descendant Martin Žužek raised olives and produced oil, presumably using the same land (Archivio di Stato di Gorizia [henceforth ASG], "Giudizio Distretto di Duino," p. 7, "1802," 17 December 1801).

22. On the serfs' obligations, see Pichler (1882: 368). Pichler, who was commissioned in about 1880 by the then owner of the castle to write its history, probably drew much of his information from the charter of 1578 but may have had other sources as well. He leaves unanswered many questions about how his employer's ancestors exploited their serfs.

23. According to Pichler (1882: 366) the Duino lords required that only the youngest son inherit. Such an inheritance system was not unheard of elsewhere (see Davis 1975: 83), but as far as I can learn from very elderly informants and from the Žužeks' practice in the Triestine Karst in the nineteenth century, it was always the oldest son who inherited the house and lands.

24. Žužek 1983–84: 52. The traveler was Johann Weikhard, Freiherr von Valvasor.

25. Cannarella 1975: 178.

26. This, I think, can reasonably be inferred from the charter of 1578, the apparent age of Slivno houses, and the nature of the land around the hamlet.

27. At the time of marriage the groom would probably have signed (made his mark on) an agreement with his father whereby the son then and there took over the family's house and land and agreed to support his parents until their deaths. On "inter-vivos" agreements between farmers and their children, see Gaunt (1983) and Berkner (1977: 400–405).

28. Pichler 1882: 152–53.

29. AST, "Urbar Herrshafft Tibein," 135.

30. Doria (1971: 10) believes that the name Vižovlje is a Slovene corruption of the Italian name for the same hamlet, Visogliano, which he believes derives from the name of a presumed Roman owner of the land.

31. Kos 1939–54: vol. 3, 206–22. So far as I know, no archaeologist has tried to learn the age of Vižovlje or any other Karst hamlet. Since Vižovlje was destroyed in World War I, its houses offer no visible clues to their age.

32. AST, "Urbar Herrschafft Tibein," 135. Žužek (1983–84: 10) agrees with the account of the founding of Vižovlje that I offer in this and the following two paragraphs.

33. Turkish raids in the area near Vižovlje began in 1469 and ended in 1527 (Bratuž et al. 1983: 40).

34. The charter of 1494 indicates that many serfs' houses were empty (Žužek 1983–84: 15–16).

35. See Ruatti (1934) and Cannarella (1975: 178–79). The Duino charter of 1578 seems to explain (p. 140r) the conditions on which peasants could settle in the fief.

36. Many Karst villages still have small stone forts or fortress-churches said to have been built for defense against the Turks. Until early in this century there was an old fortress locally called "the castle" in Sistiana, a short distance from Vižovlje. Nearby is a field called "Watch" (Straža). Perhaps it was in this "castle" or in a tower

on "Watch," rather than in the castle of Duino, that serfs from Vižovlje and other nearby hamlets did their obligatory stints of guard duty.

37. The hop hornbeam is a hardwood tree once used for tool handles and fire-wood. It flourishes even on arid, rocky land and grows back after being cut down to a stump.

38. The Church of St. Nicholas in Mavhinje conserves this census as well as reg-isters of baptisms, marriages, and funerals in Vižovlje, Mavhinje, and Cerovlje begin-ning in the 1780s.

39. Lenček 1947: 61.

40. A reader familiar with rural Yugoslavia southeast of Slovenia might wonder whether, in the seventeenth and eighteenth centuries, the Gabrovices all lived in one or more economic units organized like the traditional south Slav *zadruga*. The much-studied *zadruga* is a household composed of two or more biological families that owns the source of livelihood (usually land) jointly and regulates its work and the control of its property communally. What I have suggested is that during the period from about 1550 to 1800, the various Gabrovic families did not cluster under one (or more) roofs, *zadruga*-style, but divided the land or took up new land as fast as new households were formed. If the *zadruga* had ever been common among Slovenes, it had disappeared early in the Middle Ages. (For summaries of opinions of Slovene scholars about this, see Winner [1971: 60–64; and 1977c: 125–26].) All the old houses in the part of the Karst discussed here appear to have been built for nuclear families.

The same sort of numerical domination that we have described in Vižovlje hap-pened in some other villages. In Cerovlje, in 1813, more than half the families were named Legiša, and in Hudi log, not far off, thirteen families out of fourteen were named Pahor (AST, C.R. Gov. in Trieste, folder 1406, "Exercise 1813. . . ."). Per-haps there, too, colonizing families had multiplied while land was plentiful.

Chapter 2: Bare Survival

1. Throughout this book I do not cite my sources of information about births, marriages, places of residence, and deaths. Most of this information comes from parish and archiepiscopal records, tax lists, a will, and what I have been told by members of the Žužek and other families. Note references would have had to be many and long, and I have assumed that my readers will not need them.

2. Martin was born in 1764, and Tomaž in 1774. There was at least one more brother, Ivan, who seems to have been younger than Tomaž. Martin eventually inher-ited the Žužek house. Court records show that he was sufficiently well-off to frequently lend at interest to other farmers (ASG, "Giudizio Distretto di Duino," court records for early 1800s).

3. Blum 1948: 52–53; Blum 1978: 224.

4. According to the British social theorist Robin Fox, "In a population of be-tween three and five hundred people, after six generations or so there are only third cousins or closer to marry. During most of human history, people have lived in small, isolated communities of about that size, and have in fact been closer to the genetic equivalent of first cousins, because of their multiple consanguinity" (Shoumatoff 1985: 51).

5. Family stories and several local folk songs attest to this. One song runs: "The light is out. / The moon shines no more. / My heart aches. / . . . I will wait for my beloved. / I will stay seated by the window. / On May 12 I'll take him to [the livestock

fair at] Sežana. / I'll trade him or sell him. / I won't sell him cheap. / Because it was a job to get him. / Rather than do that I'll bring him home again / and we will make love. / My man is a good man. / He's worse than nettles. / Nettles sting anyone, / But not my man" (Merkù 1976: 41). My translation.

6. Montanelli 1905: diagram 3; Apih 1957: 83.

7. Trieste, Archivio del Catasto Fondiario, ms. "Descrizione . . . di Mauchigna . . . 1823" (a tax record).

8. On the "agglomerated" structure of many Karst villages, see M. P. Pagnini (1966: 112).

9. Lenček 1947: 61; C. Pagnini 1952: 3; Latrobe 1832: 239.

10. Trieste, Archivio del Catasto Fondiario, ms. "Descrizione . . . di Mauchigna . . . 1823."

11. Given that in the 1920s the average Slovene man on the Karst was about five feet seven inches tall (Cumin 1929: 105), and considering that factors affecting growth (nutrition and general health) were worse a century earlier, it seems likely that men in Vižovlje in the early nineteenth century would have been, on the average, even shorter than that. By contrast, American soldiers who fought in the American Revolution had a mean terminal height of five feet eight inches (Sokoloff and Villaflor 1982: 458–59). The Americans probably enjoyed a better diet, and they may have been less exposed to epidemic diseases.

12. My sources are Lenček (1947: 62) and prints and drawings.

13. Lenček 1947: 62.

14. ASG, "Giudizio Distretto di Duino," folder 3, "1830." According to Franc Žužek (1888–1978), his family used the type of beds I have described until well into the twentieth century.

15. Tomaž was bound to look after his father-in-law by the terms of agreements they made in 1809 and 1821. These two agreements resulted in Tomaž becoming the owner of his father-in-law's property while the latter was still alive (ASG, "Giudizio Distretto di Duino," p. 2, folder 2, "1822"). On "intervivos" agreements between farmers and their children, see Gaunt (1983) and Berkner (1977: 400–405).

16. Their lord at Duino may have legally owned it, while they had a hereditary right to use it and pay the lord for the privilege.

17. ASG, "Giudizio Distretto di Duino," folder 7, "Protocollo 1816," vol. 8, no. 469.

18. Ibid., no. 468.

19. Chayanov 1966; Kochanowicz 1983 and others in Wall 1983.

20. AST, I. R. Luogotenenza del Litorale, dept. 6, Commissione per la reluizione degli oneri fondiari del Litorale, temporary folder 647, fasc. 133, "Bezirk Comen—Herrschaft Duino, Gegen die Insassen von Mauchigna, Ceroule und Visoule." It is possible that in summer Tomaž and others may have paid a shepherd to pasture their sheep on Mt. Nanos, some eighteen miles away.

21. ASG, "Giudizio Distretto di Duino," folder 3, "1830."

22. AST, C.R. Gov. in Trieste, folder 1406, "Exercise 1813." For a fuller listing of the possessions of farmers in another Karst hamlet, Trebič (*treh' bich*), in 1795, see Apih (1957: 134 n. 19). Much as in Vižovlje, the average family in Trebič had a cow, an ox, and ten sheep.

23. He would have hauled the water from the Timavo River, several miles away, to the castle, or in time of drought to his livestock.

24. Their dung may have been their most important contribution to Tomaž's farming (see Homans 1941: 40).

25. Blum 1978: 280–81.

26. Le Roy Ladurie 1979: 354–55. On other medieval European peasants' work habits, see K. Thomas (1964). Peasants in nineteenth-century Hungary, both before and after they were freed from serfdom, apparently worked hard only in brief spurts (Held 1980: 21–57). Subsistence farmers in Africa are said to work in their fields about four hours a day. The figure is somewhat higher for India and much higher in the Caribbean and China (Clark and Haswell 1967: 11, 130–33). According to Chayanov (1966: 5), "the degree of [peasants'] self-exploitation is determined by a peculiar equilibrium between family demand satisfaction and the drudgery of labour itself."

27. See report by Pasquale de Ricci, 1769, in Cusin (1932: 806–10). The report deals with Karst villages nearer to Trieste than Vižovlje and three decades earlier than the period under discussion, but the description seems to fit Vižovlje farming until this century.

28. Cumin 1929.

29. I saw this happen during the summer of 1983. An eighteenth-century observer (Cusin 1932) mentions it as a frequent occurrence.

30. For this reason, no doubt, Trieste had to import most of its grain from elsewhere instead of relying on its hinterland (Cadell 1820: vol. 1, 16).

31. Apih 1957: 83.

32. Pichler 1882: 404–5, 417, 420. For a couple of anecdotes about the behavior of French soldiers in a nearby hamlet, see Schmid (1977: 37–38).

33. Perhaps this was the widespread famine of 1816–17 (Post 1976). Valentin's grandmother's grandmother was, of course, probably not a Žužek.

34. This was still true in the Karst as recently as the 1930s, as I have been told by Alberta Žužek, Maks Kočjančič, and others. The practice may be common in poor families in which the man does hard physical labor. (For other instances, see Rowntree [1922: 169 n. 1, 332].)

35. A village midwife at this time would probably have had no formal training (Shorter 1982: 35–48), and even if she had, she would have been unlikely to know anything about the danger of infection.

36. Cattle were normally watered at home or in a man-made pond in the Vižovlje common, which trapped rainfall. In time of drought water for men and beasts was hauled with considerable trouble from the Timavo River, but Vižovlje families seem to have depended mainly on their rain-filled cisterns for drinking and washing water.

37. A historian of the Russian village of Viriatino suggests that myriads of flies crawling on pacifiers were once an important vector of diseases of infants there (Benet n.d. [1970]: 121).

38. Preston and van de Walle 1978: 281.

39. "Miliary" tuberculosis, an acute form disseminated throughout the body, usually occurs in children and young people (Clark and Cumley 1973: 162). In America the death rate from all kinds of tuberculosis during the period from 1880 to 1930 was highest among "infants" zero to four years old (Frost 1940: 64).

40. See Davis (1975: 61–73, 157–75) for a discussion of how the wealthy Donà dalle Rose family of Venice in the period 1550 to 1750 apparently recognized the need to match high infant mortality with high fertility. On the related thesis that declining infant mortality in more recent times led many families to reduce fertility, see the various books in the cooperative Princeton study of the history of fertility in Europe: Coale, Anderson, and Härm (1979: chap. 3); Knodel (1974: chap. 4); Lesthaeghe (1977: chap. 5); Livi Bacci (1971: chap. 7; 1977: chap. 5); and Coale and Watkins (1986).

41. There is one minor exception. Between the births of the second Uršula in 1815 and Katarina in 1816 the elapsed time was nineteen months.

42. On lactation and temporary sterility, see Williams (1968: 482, 987–88).

43. Montanelli 1905: diagram 4; Post 1976: 21. The famine of 1816–17 extended from the British Isles to the Balkan Peninsula and was especially severe near the Karst. However, in Vižovlje—an extremely small and unreliable sample—it did not cause an unusual number of deaths.

44. ASG, Giudizio Distretto di Duino, folder 3, "1830." Late in the eighteenth century the emperors Joseph II and Leopold confirmed the right of peasants to bequeath their lands to their oldest sons. Peasants retained this legal right even after 1815, when the Hapsburgs began to require their other subjects to leave at least half of their estates to all of their children in equal shares (Strakosch 1967: 159). In Tomaž's case, what he bequeathed to Matija, in addition to personal property, was the right to use land that belonged to the della Torre family at Duino. To his two married daughters he left only the dowries they had already received.

45. That Karst men in the nineteenth century were usually in their mid-twenties when they first married is readily apparent when one looks at the marriage registers in Mavhinje and Šempolaj.

46. Among generations of Žužeks, the name Marija and variations of it recur continually and confusingly. Tomaž Žužek, with whom this chapter began, married a young woman named Marina, whose mother's name was also Marina. Tomaž's older brother married a Marija after his first wife died, and his younger brother did the same. Tomaž and Marina named both of their twin daughters Marijana, and later, after both had died, they named another daughter Marija. Their only surviving son Matija married a Marijana, and this couple named two of their four daughters Marijana. Their son Jožef[1] married a Frančiška Marija, and this couple named one of their four daughters Marija. Their son Jožef[II] married a Marija, and their son Ivan Baptist twice married women with that name. And Jožef[II] and his wife named their only daughter Marija.

47. In the next generation Jožef[II]'s wife Frančiška Marija was forty-one when she bore her last child. And in the generation after that, Jožef[III]'s wife Marija was forty-four when she had her last.

48. And one of these was Apolonija, who died a year later at twenty-one. I am not forgetting that if the marriage rate was very high, and if every family had three children who reached adult years, married, and had three children, the population would grow very fast. These conditions, of course, rarely obtained.

49. In Sweden during the years 1751 to 1800, 58 percent of boys and 61 percent of girls reached the age of twenty (Gille 1949: 36). In France, 58 percent of girls reached the age of twenty during the years 1800 to 1809. The percentage in France had been just under 50 for both boys and girls between 1782 and 1799 (Blayo 1975: 140).

50. Probably typhoid fever. In the first half of the nineteenth century, typhoid was considered a form of typhus, and it was sometimes known, for good reasons, as "putrid fever." Typhoid fever may have been endemic around Vižovlje. Matija's cousin Uršula Žužek, who lived across the road, had died of "putrid fever" a couple of years before he did. Typhoid bacteria can be spread by flies, which were not lacking in Vižovlje.

Chapter 3: The Waning of the Old Order

1. Blum's *The End of the Old Order in Rural Europe* (1978) is a magisterial survey of the decline and end of the Old Order in rural society.

2. On the role of the labor supply in peasant farming, see Clark and Haswell (1967: 126–62) and much of Chayanov's *Theory of Peasant Economy* (1966).

3. The priest may have added the nickname of Jožef[1] to distinguish him from a new neighbor and distant cousin who now lived across the road in Vižovlje and was also named Jožef Žužek. Their neighbors gave the two families unofficial "house" nicknames. As the marriage record of Jožef[1] shows, our Žužeks were dubbed "the Skittish." The new Žužeks eventually became "the Stevens" ("Šteftovi"). Our Žužeks' nickname was soon dropped, but the other Žužeks are still known by theirs.

4. This information was supplied by Franc Žužek (1888–1978), whose father had presumably told him about his upbringing. Franc maintained there had been a gradual decline in parental sternness (and filial obedience, of course) over four generations that he had heard about or observed. Of course, it is a commonplace that the old always claim, as Franc did, that children are less obedient than they once were. There is no doubt, however, that in the Žužek family and in the Karst generally, attitudes and behavior toward children did change during those generations in specific and observable ways. Parents gradually stopped insisting that children leave the house when guests were present, beat their children less, and (in the twentieth century) began to allow the children to address them as *ti* (you) rather than *vi*, which is more formal.

5. Blum 1948: 239–46. The lord of Duino at this time probably did not share the enthusiasm of other big Hapsburg landowners for a better labor force. He had very little cultivated domain land worked for him by peasants as part of their required labor service.

6. Blum 1978: 364–65; Macartney 1968: 373–75, 461–67.

7. For examples of other European emancipation myths and legends, see Du Boulay (1974: 8–9) and Winner (1971: 37–41).

8. People in the Karst hamlets near Duino claim to have seen, or to know people who have seen, the deep hole with the sharp spikes.

9. My source for this story is Elda Markuža, formerly of Vižovlje and now of Sistiana, but the tradition is well known to many in the nearby hamlets.

10. Pichler 1882: 152–53, 366.

11. If the myth does indeed deal with a historical event, is it the emancipation in 1781 or the ending of subjection, manorial dues, and labor services in 1848? Here is a scrap of evidence on the matter. Elda Markuža, whose version of the myth I have related, says that she has always been told that a count of Duino (perhaps the villain of the story) might, if he had wished, have enjoyed the "first night" with her great-great-grandmother but declined to do so because she was too homely. A calculation of the probable decade of the woman's marriage would suggest that the counts were still (within the reality of the myth) enjoying their privilege in about 1840, and therefore that the myth has its origin in the events of 1848. On the other hand, Joseph II's emancipation decree of 1781 and related tax reform did inspire a great deal of peasant violence in the Hapsburg lands. It is easier to imagine a myth of violent peasant protest over a murdered girl developing around that emancipation than around the decree of 1848.

12. AST, I. R. Luogotenenza del Litorale, dept. 6, Commissione per la reluizione degli oneri fondiari del Litorale, temporary folder no. 647, fasc. 133, "Bezirk Comen—Herrschaft Duino Gegen die Insassen von Mauchigna, Ceroule und Visoule." For a very brief legal and institutional history of the area around Vižovlje, see a typewritten manuscript on file at the Archivio di Stato di Trieste called "Riordinamento degli usi civici delle frazioni di Malchina, Visogliano, Sistiana e Ceroglie dell'Ermada—Relazione generale," especially pp. 16–22.

13. In the parish registers of marriages at Mavhinje there are notations concerning completed military service after about 1875.

14. Žužek 1983–84: 60.

15. For some comments on under classes in south central Europe and especially on the way language is often associated with inferior status, see Wolff (1956: 150) and Lokar (1977: 54–56).

16. The direct line of the della Torre family had recently died out. The castle of Duino and its lands were then inherited by a cousin, the princess. Her heir was succeeded by a prince of Thurn und Taxis, whose descendants are still the owners. In the 1920s they resumed the use of the Italian form of their name, and the present owner is called Prince Della Torre e Tasso. Local people persist in referring to him as Prince Thurn und Taxis.

17. Lutyens 1965: 194.

18. Ibid.: 267, 273, 278, 291.

Chapter 4: Ripple Effects

1. On the views of Alexander Gerschenkron and W. W. Rostow and on more recent interpretations, see Trebilcock (1981: chapters 1 and 6).

2. For examples of the gradualist interpretation of Austro-Hungarian industrialization, see Matis and Bachinger (1973), and especially the recent book by Good (1984), which also provides a useful discussion of the historiography of the subject.

3. Paton 1849: vol. 2, 214.

4. Luzzatto Fegiz 1929: 16.

5. For a detailed study of changes in farming in a few inland villages, see Moritsch (1969).

6. These are cited in Chapter 3.

7. Every summer, however, hired shepherds took the sheep of the Karst hamlets to mountain pastures eighteen miles from Vižovlje (Caharija 1975–76).

8. Cadell 1820: vol. 1, 16.

9. I assume that the family's practice at this time was the same as it was later, in 1900, when they ate almost no meat.

10. For my description of the Žužeks' farming at this time I am relying partly on information provided by Franc Žužek and Lojza Legiša, although their memories extended back only to about 1900. I have no reason to think there were any important changes in the late nineteenth-century decades except for the abandoning of sheep raising and (perhaps) alterations in the family's division of the farm labor. Both of these are discussed later in this chapter.

11. Farmers began to grow potatoes in significant amounts in the southwestern Hapsburg lands soon after the disastrous grain crop failures of 1816–17. As late as 1875, farmers in the area that roughly corresponds to the Triestine Karst planted potatoes on only 4.5 percent of their cultivated fields, but a little more than half a century later they grew potatoes on a fifth of their fields (Blaznik, Grafenauer, and Vilfan 1970: 265, 269).

12. Merkù 1976: 49.

13. Minnich (1979) deals at length with the present-day rituals of pig slaughtering in another Slovene village.

14. A similar division of labor was common throughout much of Europe, and in many places it changed as men and women entered the industrial economy. For a few comments about the division of labor in the Karst, see Cumin (1929: 107). For villages elsewhere, see Le Roy Ladurie (1979: 354); Benet (n.d. [1970]: 14, 95); and Halpern (1958: 69–71). More general discussion may be found in Scott and Tilly

(1975: 145–78). In another work, the same authors stress how hard farm women worked (Tilly and Scott 1978: 44–47).

15. These occasions made a great impression on the mind of the little Franc Žužek, who recalled them vividly as an old man.

16. Information from Franc Žužek and others.

17. Hočevar (1965: 50) suggests that the agrarian reforms may have had this and other effects in Slovenia.

18. Cumin 1929; Žužek 1983–84: 19.

19. It was common for nineteenth-century small-scale farming to merge into industrial work (for central and eastern Europe, see Blum 1978: 299), and the pattern survives. For Yugoslavia in the 1970s, see Lockwood (1976: 281–300, esp. 286).

20. Carting was often the first work that farmers undertook on the margins of industry. See Benet (n.d. [1970]: 29) for the same pattern in a Russian village in the 1860s.

21. We do not know how much time Jožef[1] had to spend on labor services, if any, or how much time he devoted to producing food and earning money to pay his manorial dues. In the early nineteenth century, peasants in the village of Žerovnica, not many miles from Vižovlje, still had to perform fourteen days of labor service a year (Winner 1971: 40). Aleš Lokar, professor of economics at the Università degli studi di Urbino, Italy, who has helped me with the research on this book in many ways, believes that the labor services before 1848 were not heavy enough to interfere with industrial work. The problem, he maintains, is that there was no industrial work to do.

22. Caharija 1975–76: 20–21; Cumin 1929: 93–94.

23. Jožef Kravanja ("Matijevi").

24. Golab 1973: 213.

25. On the problems of farmers and European peasants in adjusting to American industrial life, see Hareven (1981: chap. 6) and Gutman (1976: 3–30). On the adjustment in Europe, see Pollard (1963); Thompson (1967); and Stearns (1975: 163).

26. Franklin Mendels has pointed out (1972: 241) that in the first stages of industrialization, rural industries, especially textile industries, often provide work in the farmers' slack season, thus putting people to work on a more continuous basis. This was not true of marble quarrying.

27. In Indian villages in the 1970s, farmers' authority over their sons is said to be weakening as economic development takes place, although the precise reasons for weakening are not the ones I have discussed here (Kessinger 1974: 196; Caldwell, Reddy, and Caldwell 1982: 715).

28. The revisionist view, however, is that in traditional European and American farm families, women had bigger economic roles and more power than historians used to think was the case. See Scott and Tilly (1975); Shorter (1975: 66–73 and notes); and Lerner (1971: 16–19).

29. Minchinton (1973: 113) summarizes current opinion in this way: "What was true of Britain was true of other countries too. Once the initial phase of industrialization was over, real incomes began to rise."

30. Most of the houses in Vižovlje, including the Žužeks', were shelled to the ground in World War I, rebuilt, gutted by fire in World War II, and then rebuilt again. The repeated destruction and rebuilding makes it impossible to reconstruct from the evidence of the existing house what was done to it during the nineteenth century. But I do know, from conversations with Franc Žužek, what the house was like on the eve of World War I, and I have some information (see note 31 below) from tax records and informants about the way people in Vižovlje changed their roofs in the nineteenth

century. Studies of domestic architecture in the Karst (Nice 1940; M. P. Pagnini 1966) and the dates carved on gateways and cisterns in other hamlets make it fairly clear when many Karst homeowners raised the roofs of their houses and made other improvements.

31. I suspect that in the eighteenth century all the houses had roofs of fieldstone. Replacement with tiles probably began in the early nineteenth century, especially if the hamlet was burned during the Napoleonic wars. By 1823, eight houses had tile roofs and five had stone ones (Trieste, Archivio del Catasto Fondiario, ms., "Descrizione . . . di Mauchigna . . . 1823"). By the eve of World War I, I have been told, all the houses but one in Vižovlje had tile roofs.

32. At this same time, peasants in the Russian village of Viriatino were enabled by their mild prosperity to modernize their one-room log huts, which they shared with their animals. They rebuilt using bricks for walls and tin for roofs; made the houses bigger, with several rooms; added bathhouses nearby; and built sheds for the animals and moved them out of the houses (Benet n.d. [1970]: 58–73).

33. It can be made out in a real estate map of 1892.

34. In antiquity the Roman empress Livia, wife of Augustus, is said to have loved a "Pucinum" wine produced somewhere near Vižovlje. Thanks to the fact that she drank it regularly, it is said, she lived to the age of about eighty-four.

35. Genovese 1972: 63.

36. Fogel and Engerman 1974: 90–99; David et al. 1976: 231–301. I have used Fogel and Engerman's information about whites' diet and Sutch's about blacks'.

37. The informant was Ivan Blažina. Lack of food and abundance of work produced a lean people. This influenced the male ideal of female beauty. In the Trieste area there is an old saying: "Women are like fritters; they're no good unless they're round and a little fat."

38. For a discussion of the same considerations in another poor rural community without a social security system, see Du Boulay (1974: 21).

Chapter 5: Surplus People

1. On the role of medicine versus the roles of sanitation and the rising standard of living, see the conclusions of McKeown (1976: 152–54), and Preston and van de Walle (1978: 291). On the decline of mortality in Italy, see Hoffman (1981).

2. The third floor may have been added by an earlier generation, however.

3. Some historians have suggested that the diffusion of the potato, so easily grown and so nutritious, was largely responsible for Europe's initial population explosion (see especially Langer [1963]). Fogel tentatively suggests that "improvements in nutritional status may have accounted for as much as four tenths of the decline in mortality rates [in Europe and America since 1800], but nearly all of this effect was concentrated in the reduction of infant mortality" (Fogel 1984: Abstract).

4. They did not draw their water from a well, or a river in a populous area, two water sources that are easily polluted with fecal matter, but from cisterns of rainwater, or occasionally from the unpolluted Timavo River. One might therefore assume that they were less likely to suffer from diarrhea, cholera, and other waterborne diseases than children in the towns. (On urban mortality from dysentery, see especially Preston and van de Walle [1978], and on the connecton between sanitation and nutrition, see Hoffman [1981: 106–9].) Nevertheless, at least four Žužek children in three

nineteenth-century generations died of dysentery, and many of the other early childhood deaths that the priest called "weakness" and "ordinary" and "natural" may have had the same cause.

5. Marija Colja was the Vižovlje midwife in the first half of the twentieth century. According to her daughter she received some instruction in obstetrics in Trieste.

6. Evelyn Ackerman (1978: 56) analyzes the way notions of hygiene might have reached a French village in the middle of the nineteenth century. Trained midwives, education that touched on health matters, and even doctors may have played a role. These three forces probably came into play on the Karst only in the early twentieth century.

7. The Žužeks, according to Franc and Elda Žužek, rarely had any medical care from a doctor until the mid-1930s.

8. With santonin and other vermifuges.

9. Pavla Žužek ("Kržankni").

10. Franc Žužek and others.

11. What was happening at about this same time in the farm village of Viriatino in Russia is instructive. Young peasants and laborers were starting to defy their parents and marry whom they chose. Prosperity and a wider range of possible jobs may have helped to bring this about (Benet n.d. [1970]: 107).

12. My source of information is her granddaughter, Elda Marcuža.

13. True, even a century earlier more than one child in a family was likely to survive childhood. We obviously cannot know whether Karlina would have survived childhood in a period of higher mortality.

14. Lojza Legiša of Vižovlje (1896–1982), formerly of Medja vas, was a milkmaid in the years just prior to World War I and described this daily routine to me. Her daily round trip to Trieste was some twenty-eight miles long.

15. Recollections of Lojza Legiša (1896–1982) and Ivan Blažina (1890–).

16. See Chapter 4.

17. On Slovene migration to Trieste and settlement in its blue-collar suburbs, see Arnez (1983: 290–93).

18. For discussions by historians of the difficulty of this adjustment, see Weber's still provocative *Growth of Cities* (1899), especially chapters 7 and 8; Handlin's classic *The Uprooted* (1951); Chatelain (1976: chap. 2, 1061–79); and Hohenberg and Lees (1985: chap. 9). For remarks by an anthropologist on this problem as peasants today experience it all over the world, see Potter, Diaz, and Foster (1967: 379).

19. AST, Trib. Prov. Atti Criminali, 1850–1923, folder 5751, p. 1871, and folder 3373, sheaf 176.

20. Ibid., folder 3529, p. 179.

21. Hanagan has suggested (1980: 75–76) that much drinking by urban laborers in this period may have resulted from their having, for the first time, enough money to buy alcohol.

Chapter 6: A Peasant in the Machine Age

1. According to one of the sons, Franc Žužek (1888–1978), when he was a boy the family owned thirteen separate pieces of woodlot, pasture, and cultivated land. There is no reason to think these thirteen pieces were not the same thirty-six acres that their ancestors had used when they were serfs of the Duino lords, and that became their own property, outright, in 1861.

2. The existence at this point of a shoemaker in Mavhinje is suggestive of the Karst's nineteenth-century development, modest though it was. In 1813 the only shoemaker in the area was at Duino (Žužek 1983–84: 65).

3. For a summary of the history of the abolition of entails and primogeniture in Austria and northern Italy, see Davis (1975: 139–45), and for other areas, see works cited in that book on p. 75, n. 4.

4. According to his brother Franc, no one contested Jožef''''s inheritance of the house and land. An Austrian law of the eighteenth century permitted peasants who made wills to leave everything to one heir, in spite of the general law requiring all other subjects to divide at least half of their estates among all of their children (*Österreichisches Recht* 1968–71: vol. 1, art. 761; Strakosch 1967: 159).

5. Early in the twentieth century, Franc told me, a Karst farmhouse and enough land to farm cost about a thousand florins.

6. Homans suggests (1941: 131–39, 215) that this must usually have happened in medieval England.

7. I say this on the basis of the appearance of his house (see Fig. 12) and what I have been told by one of his sons.

8. Some of my information about Valentin's early life was supplied by Jožef Kravanja ("Matijevi") and other contemporaries, but most was told me by my father-in-law, Franc Žužek. Franc was a truthful man, but he cordially disliked his brother, and this may have colored what he told me. I regret that I never asked Valentin to tell me his own life story. Given his hostile relationship with my father-in-law, however, such a discussion would have been difficult, and by the time I knew that I was going to write this history, Valentin was senile.

9. Genesis: 25. 29–34; 27. 1–4.

10. On the way Polish peasants traditionally taught their children, see Galeski (1976: 233).

11. Žužek 1983–84: 168.

12. On Austrian educational policy in Slovenia, see Čepič et al. (1979: 432 and 548–52).

13. By 1900 a little more than half of the people of Vižovlje could read (Žužek 1983–84: 205).

14. Not far away, in Slovenia (Yugoslavia), "those peasants who went to work in factories in the period between the world wars were looked down upon by their fellow villagers. . . . To be a prosperous farmer was considered a point of pride" (Halpern 1963: 171).

15. On the modernization of Hungarian agriculture and its impact on peasant life, see Held (1980: 57–90, 197–317).

16. On the introduction into the Karst of Swiss cattle and Yorkshire pigs, both developed in the previous century in England, see Società Alpina (1909: 22–24).

17. Schmid 1977: 66 n. 65.

18. Potter, Diaz, and Foster 1967: 317.

19. Near the end of Valentin's life, Danilo Terčon, who in 1938 was a teen-ager from another hamlet, confessed to having been the cherry thief. He had not known that it was his deed that had triggered the four decades of hostility between the brothers.

20. Potter, Diaz, and Foster 1967: 297.

21. Franc Žužek, Lojza Žužek, Agostin Blažina, Pavla Žužek, Lojza Legiša.

22. So it seemed to Valentin's nieces, his brother Franc's children.

Chapter 7: Slots for Proletarians

1. This movement is in part the subject matter of Handlin (1951); Chatelain (1976); and Lees (1979).

2. On the continuum between farm and factory in modern Yugoslavia, see Lockwood (1976: 286).

3. Education might have qualified these boys for another traditional career besides farming: the priesthood. It was not unusual for a well-behaved lad who excelled in school to be recommended to a seminary by his village priest. The early life of Father Stanislao Žerjal, who in the 1970s was the aged priest of the churches of Slivno and Šempolaj, illustrates the typical pattern. The son of a farmer in nearby Komen, in his teens he was a brilliant pupil and a lazy farm boy. According to his sisters, when his parents needed him for hoeing, weeding, or cutting wood he hid in the hayloft and read. When a decision had to be made about his future, therefore, his parents did the logical thing and encouraged him to become a priest. Presumably Emil and Franc did not shine brightly enough in the little Mavhinje school to be singled out as promising clerics, and Emil, as this chapter will show, definitely lacked the temperament for the job.

4. My source of information about Emil's life was his stepdaughter, Roberta Crisman. She hated even the memory of him, and I have tried to filter from her recollections only what seemed to be the reasonably certain facts of his life.

5. Cankar 1930: 18. As we shall see, Emil did occasionally turn up in and around Vižovlje.

6. Ožbalt 1981: 61–62.

7. Ibid., 62–64. The stories are "Polikarp," "Smrt in pogreb Jakoba Nesreče" [The death and burial of Jacob Nesreče], "Aleš iz Razor" [Alex of Razor], and "Jure" [George].

8. Needless to say, my major source of information about his life was Franc himself.

9. See chapter 6.

10. Marx and Engels 1967: 84.

11. For a couple of decades after the war, local farmers supplemented their incomes by selling the shell fragments they found in their fields as scrap iron.

12. Typhus viruses are carried from one human victim to another by lice. In the first year of World War I many people in the northern Karst died of typhus. Does this mean that most of these peasants and laborers ordinarily were lousy? To judge by what I know about attitudes and behavior in Vižovlje two decades later, I would guess not. In the 1930s the local schoolteacher sent children home if they were found to be lousy, and parents tried to keep their children free of lice. Milka Žužek, Valentin's daughter, was only three years old when her mother died, but she vividly recalls that while her aunt was dressing her for the funeral she discovered that Milka was lousy and cut off all her hair. There was, however, one family in Vižovlje whose children were often and notoriously lousy, and wandering beggars (see Chapter 9) were often crawling with lice. No doubt in wartime, when many were driven from their homes and took refuge together crowded into sheds and barns in other hamlets, such a family or such a beggar served as the pool from which lice spread, infesting most of the refugees and preparing the way for an epidemic.

13. Valentin was exempted, as was mentioned earlier, because from birth he had lacked the fingertips on his right hand needed for firing a rifle.

14. In 1794 Vižovlje consisted of fourteen families. In 1945 the number in the old

part of the hamlet was still fourteen, but there were now a handful of others scattered along the road between Vižovlje and Sistiana.

15. Cumin 1929: 223.

16. Lojza's mother and paternal grandmother came from Mavhinje and Šempolaj, however.

Chapter 8: Becoming Modern

1. For a fuller discussion of modernization, see below.

2. Poster conserved at Kulturni Dom, Trieste.

3. Mihelič 1969: 35.

4. Poster at Kulturni Dom, Trieste.

5. On Fascist Italianization in and around Trieste, see Rusinow (1969: 199–207); Kacin-Wohinz (1972); Pirjevec's summary in Pirjevec 1983a; Parovel (1985).

6. On one occasion when Mussolini passed through Sistiana in a motorcade on his way to Trieste, the local schoolchildren, including Franc's offspring, were taken to cheer him, just as Franc and his schoolmates had been taken a generation earlier to greet Emperor Francis Joseph. Most of the small crowd of Slovenes and Italians by the roadside yelled "Duce!" which in Italian means "Leader!" but in the local Slovene dialect sounds like two words, "Du če?" which mean "Who wants?" To the mortification of their Italian teacher, the Slovene children yelled "Nočem!" which means "I don't want!"

7. Wolff 1956: 152. See also Lokar and Thomas (1977: 29–30). There had been no significant emigration from the Trieste area in the nineteenth or early twentieth centuries.

8. For a careful psychosociological study of present-day relations between language groups in northeastern Italy, and especially of attitudes toward the use of different languages, see Sussi's article in Davis et al. (1983: 176–85).

9. Arnez (1958: 24), quoting from Mario Alberti, *L'irredentismo senza romanticismi* (Como, 1936), p. 350.

10. On Italian motives, see Rusinow (1969) and Kacin-Wohinz (1972 and 1977).

11. Cardoza's recent study of fascism in the Bologna countryside (1982) begins with an up-to-date review of the historical literature on the role of the elites, especially rural ones, in the rise of the movement. For a skeptical examination of the connections between Italian fascism and the industrialists, see Melograni (1972).

12. See the essay of Aleš Lokar in Pirjevec (1983b: 119–29, esp. 128).

13. Archivio della Curia Arcivescovile di Gorizia, Visitazioni, 93, "Malchina," 6 Sept. 1929.

14. Concerning Slovene emigration to the United States, see Winner (1977a and 1977b); Susel (1977); and Molek (1978).

15. This was the same Anton Klarič who, some years earlier, had captured his future wife's heart when she saw him whistling on his way to work (see Chapter 5).

16. Rogers 1969: 14; DeWalt 1979: 9.

17. The pig was fattened for slaughter in the fall and conversion into ham and sausages.

18. A working man was thought to need hot food. See Fig. 5, which shows a quarry worker eating the lunch his wife has brought him.

19. Scott and Tilly (1975).

20. On the decline of fertility, especially in rural areas, see Behrman, Corsa, and Freedman (1969), historical articles by Coale, Glass, Kirk, Ryder, Easterlin, and Kuznets; Coale (1975); Biraben (1966); Eversley (1959); and C. Tilly (1978). Coale and Watkins (1986), is a book-length survey of the discoveries of a series of studies of the European fertility decline that reports much of what is now known about the motives for the decline. For a skeptical view of a finding concerning a possible connection between declining infant mortality and declining fertility, see Matthiessen and Mc-Cann (1978).

21. Luzzatto Fegiz 1929: 51–53.

22. Ibid., p. 51.

23. In north Italy in 1931, the association of male literacy with low or declining fertility was relatively high and statistically significant at the .01 level (Livi Bacci 1977: 197 and Table 5.5).

24. He was away for a fairly long period during the 1930s when he was building roads in the Istrian Peninsula and for another in the early 1940s when he was building air-raid shelters for German troops at Sežana.

25. Hočevar 1979: 185–86.

Chapter 9: Costs of War

1. Milward 1977: chaps. 2 and 9.

2. Marwick 1974: 112–32, 192–94.

3. Clough 1964: 279, 286; Corbino 1962: 312–14. Because of poor data, changes in the value of the lira, and problems in assessing damages, these figures are only approximate.

4. It seems clear that food was more plentiful in the country than in the cities in Vichy France and Germany. In Russia, perhaps, there was as much starvation in the one as in the other (Marwick 1974: 120, 125–27, 135, 193).

5. When they ate meat, many adults sent their children out of the house. (Danilo Terčon of Sistiana, Maks Kočjančič of Cerovlje, and others have told me this.)

6. On similar remedies used in other Karst villages, see Merkù (1976: 52, 91–92).

7. Maks Kočjančič of Cerovlje, Lojza Žužek's nephew, tells me that numerous people in his hamlet died of tuberculosis in the 1930s and early 1940s without ever having been treated by a doctor.

8. Their ability to read, which was new in Franc's generation, may also have made them aware of wealth and poverty.

9. The schoolteacher, however, as we have seen, was an instrument of the Mussolini government's harsh program of Italianization.

10. At this time none of the Žužeks smoked.

11. Mervic-Legiša and Furlan 1970.

12. These small bands were constantly on the move to avoid encirclement (Novak 1970: 61–62).

13. Mervic-Legiša and Furlan 1970.

14. Seven women from Vižovlje, however, served as partisan "activists" or "territorials," spying, providing food and information, and organizing clandestine meetings (Mervic-Legiša and Furlan 1970).

15. Fearing that their hamlet might be burned, they had earlier hidden some belongings in a narrow crevasse behind the house. One thing they thus saved was Franc and Lojza's wool mattress.

16. During much of this day, Milka Žužek, Valentin's daughter, hid in a small rabbit hutch close to the courtyard where the other young women were being collected. Though she was only poorly concealed by some leaves and rags, and soldiers often stood and chatted near the hutch, they never discovered her.

17. On the movements of the New Zealanders, see Cox (1947: 193; 1977: 186).

Chapter 10: Tarnished Miracle

1. For a thoughtful discussion of the European boom, see Postan (1967: pt. 1).

2. Caracciolo (1969: 180–83) credits several factors for Italy's postwar industrial development, especially the breaking of protectionist, social, and cultural barriers to trade with Europe, the United States, and the rest of the world. For a bibliography on the "Italian miracle," see Consiglio Regionale della Toscana (1978: 96–127).

3. Trieste has not prospered as much as many other Italian cities, despite the city's efforts to improve its port facilities and its links with eastern Europe. Nevertheless there was a very marked rise in employment and the standard of living during the 1950s and 1960s (Mihelič 1969: 13–29, 51).

4. In the 1970s, however, the Karst quarries suffered from competition with other Italian marbles and with other building materials such as granite. See Lokar's comments in Davis et al. (1983: 170–72).

5. Caharija 1975–76: 106. There might have been even more jobs and higher pay for the indigenous population if there had not been large additions to the local labor force. After World War II, numerous Italian-speaking Yugoslavs migrated to Italy and settled in the northwestern Karst, where they competed with the local people for jobs.

6. Lokar and Oblak 1983: 13–14. See also Lokar's comments in Davis et al. (1983: 172–74).

7. To this day many Karst hamlets across the border in Yugoslavia have no public water supply. Each family traps its rainwater in a cistern.

8. Clough 1964: 360–61.

9. By the 1970s, only Valentin's son Bruno and one other man in Vižovlje made their livings solely by farming. Even in the hamlets of Mavhinje and Slivno, a little farther than Vižovlje from the highway and the city, less than a tenth of the fifty or so families made their livings solely by farming (Caharija 1975–76: 64). Of course not everyone completely abandoned agriculture. Here, and all across south central Europe, some farmers instead drifted toward areas with better soil, higher farm wages, or better markets for their crops. Retired police colonel Abramo Schmid told me in the spring of 1980 of a conversation he had had with a Slovene who owns Karst farmland not far from Vižovlje. Rather than work his own rocky land, the man told him, he worked as a day laborer for a farmer in the much richer Italian province of Friuli, a little to the west of his own land. Was his own land unused? Schmid asked this Slovene. No, he answered, a Serbian from deep in central Yugoslavia rented and worked his land. Well, Schmid wondered, did the Serb own land, and if so, who worked it? The two men went and asked him, and the Serb responded that he did indeed own a farm and that it was rented and worked by a Rumanian.

10. Some of the new homeowners, however, were Slovenes who had sold their fields and pastures to Triestines and used the proceeds to build houses for themselves.

11. The history of the Žužeks' living arrangements in the nineteenth and twentieth centuries seems to accord with the old belief, recently under attack by Peter Laslett and others, that most European families used to be extended and only became nuclear under the impact of industrialization. For a convenient summary of the historians' argument on this point, see Vinovskis (1977).

12. Under Italian law (Bruno 1923: articles 736, 805, 806, 899) he could legally have bequeathed five eighths of his property to Angelo (half of it plus a quarter—there being four siblings—of the other half). By the 1970s I would guess most testators on the Karst divided their property equally among their children.

13. Franc's views, as stated in this and the following six paragraphs, are those he expressed from time to time if asked.

14. Not only better nutrition but also greater control of disease may have caused children to grow taller. In the 1920s the average Slovene man on the Karst was about five feet seven inches tall (Cumin 1929: 105). There are no data on the height of the same group in the post–World War II period, but the height of the average Italian recruit (Italian- or Slovene-speaking) in the Friuli-Venezia Giulia region in the mid-1970s was about five feet nine inches (Italy. Istituto Centrale di Statistica 1979: 10). I would guess that the Slovene recruits were as tall as the Italian ones.

15. Loss of the village sense of community is a familiar theme in village studies. On the reasons for this, see Galeski (1976: 245, 346); Homans (1950: 334–68); and Du Boulay (1974: 249).

16. By contrast, in the Serbian village that Joel Halpern first studied in 1958, old men were "still looked upon as the preservers of tradition and [were] eagerly listened to by young people" (Halpern 1967: 21). That village had undergone less social change than Vižovlje, so perhaps the younger people had less scorn for the past.

Bibliography

Ackerman, Evelyn. 1978. *Village on the Seine: Tradition in Bonnières, 1815–1914.* Ithaca, N.Y.

Adamček, Josip. 1968. *Seljačka buna 1573* [The peasant uprising of 1573]. Donja Stubica, Yugoslavia.

————. 1980. *Agrarni odnosi u Hrvatskoj od sredine xv do kraja xvii stolječa* [Agrarian conditions in Croatia from the middle of the fifteenth to the end of the seventeenth century]. Zagreb.

Apih, Elio. 1957. *La società triestina nel secolo xviii.* Trieste.

Arnez, John A. 1958. *Slovenia in European Affairs.* New York.

————. 1983. *Slovenian Lands and their Economies, 1848–1873.* New York.

Beardsley, Richard K., John W. Hall, and Robert E. Ward. 1959. *Village Japan.* Chicago.

Behrman, Samuel J., Leslie Corsa, and Ronald Freedman, et al. 1969. *Fertility and Family Planning.* Ann Arbor.

Bell, Rudolph M. 1979. *Fate and Honor, Family and Village: Demographic and Cultural Change in Italy Since 1800.* Chicago.

Benet, Sula, ed. and trans. N.d. [1970]. *The Village of Viriatino: An Ethnographical Study of a Russian Village from before the Revolution to the Present.* Garden City, N.Y.

Berend, Ivan T., and György Ranki. 1982. *The European Periphery and Industrialization, 1780–1914.* Cambridge, England.

Berkner, Lutz K. 1977. "The Stem Family and the Developmental Cycle of the Peasant Household: An Eighteenth Century Austrian Example." *American Historical Review* 77: 398–418.

Biraben, Jean-Noël. 1966. "Evolution de la fécondité en Europe occidentale de l'époque prémalthusien à l'époque actuelle." In Council of Europe, *European Population Conference,* vol. 1, 17–27. Strasbourg.

Blayo, Ivo. 1975. "La mortalité en France de 1740 à 1829." *Population* 30 (special issue): 123–42.

Blaznik, Pavle, Bogo Grafenauer, and S. Vilfan, eds. 1970. *Gospodarska in družbena zgodovina Slovencev* [Economic and social history of the Slovenes]. Vol. 1. Ljubljana.

Blum, Jerome. 1948. *Noble Landowners and Agriculture in Austria, 1815–1848.* Baltimore.

———. 1978. *The End of the Old Order in Rural Europe.* Princeton.

Blythe, Ronald. 1970. *Akenfield: Portrait of an English Village.* New York.

Bratuž, Lojzka, Aleš Brecelj, Ivan Kretič, et al. 1983. *Devin dom Lepe Vide po spominih in zgodovinskih virih* [Duino, the home of Lepa Vida, based on recollections and historical sources]. Duino, Italy.

Bruno, A., ed. 1923. *Codice civile del Regno d'Italia.* Florence.

Brusatti, Alois, ed. 1973. *Die Habsburger Monarchie 1848–1918.* Vol. 1, *Die wirtschaftliche Entwicklung.* Vienna.

Cadell, W. A. 1820. *A Journey in Carniola, Italy, and France in the Years 1817, 1818.* 2 vols. Edinburgh.

Caharija, Vera. 1975–76. "Il comune di Duino-Aurisina. Uno studio di geografia umana." Laurea thesis, University of Trieste.

Caldwell, John C., P. H. Reddy, and Pat Caldwell. 1982. "The Causes of Demographic Change in Rural South India: A Micro Approach." *Population and Development Review* 8:689–727.

Cankar, Ivan. 1930. *The Bailiff Yerney and His Rights.* Translated by Sidonie Yeras and H. C. Sewell Grant. London.

Cannarella, Dante. 1959. *Il Carso e la sua preistoria.* Trieste.

———. 1968. *Il Carso. Invito alla conoscenza della sua preistoria, della sua storia, delle sue bellezze.* Trieste.

———. 1975. *Guida del Carso triestino: Preistoria, storia, natura.* Trieste.

———. 1980. "Discendiamo dai pugliesi?" *La Bora* (Trieste) 4: 17–21.

Caracciolo, Alberto. 1969. "Il processo d'industrializzazione." In *Lo sviluppo economico in Italia,* edited by Giorgio Fuà, vol. 3, 96–183. Milan.

Cardoza, Anthony L. 1982. *Agrarian Elites and Italian Fascism: the Province of Bologna, 1901–1926.* Princeton.

Čepič, Zdenko, Ferdo Gestrin, Bogo Grafenauer, et al. 1979. *Zgodovina Slovencev* [History of the Slovenes]. Ljubljana.

Chatelain, Abel. 1976. *Les migrants temporaires en France de 1800 à 1914.* 2 vols. Lille.

Chayanov, A. V. 1966. *A. V. Chayanov on the Theory of Peasant Economy.* Edited by Daniel Thorner, Bruce Kerblay, and R. E. F. Smith. Homewood, Ill.

Clark, Colin, and Margaret Haswell. 1967. *The Economics of Subsistence Agriculture.* 3d ed. New York.

Clark, Randolph L., and Russell W. Cumley, eds. 1973. *The Book of Health: a Medical Encyclopedia for Everyone.* New York.

Clough, Shepard B. 1964. *The Economic History of Modern Italy.* New York.

Coale, Ansley J., Jr., ed. 1975. *Economic Factors in Population Growth.* New York.

———, Barbara A. Anderson, and Erna Härm. 1979. *Human Fertility in Russia since the Nineteenth Century.* Princeton.

Coale, Ansley J., Jr., and Susan C. Watkins. 1986. *The Decline of Fertility in Europe.* Princeton.

Collomp, Alain. 1983. *La maison du père. Famille et village en Haute-Provence aux XVIIe et XVIIIe siècles.* Paris.

Consiglio Regionale della Toscana. 1978. *L'Italia negli ultimi trent'anni.* Florence.

Corbino, Epicarmo. 1962. *L'economia italiana dal 1860 al 1960.* Bologna.

Cox, Geoffrey. 1947. *The Road to Trieste*. London.

———. 1977. *The Race for Trieste*. London.

Cumin, Gustavo. 1929. *Guida della Carsia Giulia*. Trieste.

Cusin, Fabio. 1932. *Le condizioni giuridico e economiche dell'agro triestino nel sec. xviii*. Trieste.

———. 1937. *Il confine orientale d'Italia nella politica europea del xiv e xv secolo*. 2 vols. Milan.

David, Paul A., Herbert G. Gutman, Richard Sutch, Peter Temin, and Gavin Wright. 1976. *Reckoning with Slavery: A Critical Study in the Quantitative History of American Negro Slavery*. New York.

Davis, James C. 1975. *A Venetian Family and Its Fortune, 1500–1900: The Donà and the Conservation of Their Wealth*. Philadelphia.

———. 1976. "A Slovene Laborer and His Experience of Industrialization, 1888–1976." *East European Quarterly* 10: 3–19.

Davis, James C., Jože Pirjevec, Aleš Lokar, and Emidio Sussi. 1983. "Symposium: The Slovenes of Northeastern Italy." *Nationalities Papers* 11: 148–89.

DeWalt, Billie R. 1979. *Modernization in a Mexican Ejido: A Study in Economic Adaptation*. Cambridge, England.

Doria, Mario. 1971. *Alla ricerca di toponomi prelatini nel Carso*. Trieste.

Du Boulay, Juliet. 1974. *Portrait of a Greek Mountain Village*. Oxford.

Easterlin, Richard A. 1976a. "Factors in the Decline of Farm Family Fertility in the United States: Some Preliminary Research Results." *Journal of American History* 63: 600–614.

———. 1976b. "Population Change and Farm Settlement in the United States." *Journal of Economic History* 36: 45–75.

Edwards, R. Dudley, and T. Desmond Williams, eds. 1956. *The Great Famine: Studies in Irish History, 1845–52*. Dublin.

Eversley, D. E. C. 1959. *Social Theories of Fertility and the Malthusian Debate*. Oxford.

Flinn, Michael W. 1981. *The European Demographic System*. Baltimore.

Fogel, Robert W. 1984. *Nutrition and the Decline in Mortality since 1700: Some Preliminary Findings*. National Bureau of Economic Research Working Paper No. 1402. Cambridge, Mass.

Fogel, Robert W., and Stanley L. Engerman. 1974. *Time on the Cross: Evidence and Methods—A Supplement*. Boston.

Frost, Wade Hampton. 1940. "The Age Selection of Mortality from Tuberculosis in Successive Decades." *Millbank Memorial Fund Quarterly* 18: 61–66.

Galeski, Boguslaw. 1976. "Determinants of Rural Social Change: Sociological Problems of the Contemporary Polish Village." In *The Social Structure of Eastern Europe*, edited by Bernard L. Faber, 229–58. New York.

Gaspari, Paolo. 1976. *Storia popolare della società contadina in Friuli: Agricoltura e società rurale in Friuli dal x al xx secolo*. Monza.

Gaunt, David. 1983. "The property and kin relationships of retired farmers in northern and central Europe." In *Family Forms in Historic Europe*, edited by Richard Wall. Cambridge, England.

Genicot, Leopold. 1966. "Crisis: from the Middle Ages to Modern Times." In *The Cambridge Economic History of Europe from the Decline of the Roman Empire*, 2d ed., edited by J. H. Clapham and Eileen Power. Vol. 1, 660–741. Cambridge, England.

Genovese, Eugene D. 1972. *Roll, Jordan, Roll. The World the Slaves Made*. New York and Toronto.

Gille, H. 1949. "The Demographic History of the Northern European Countries in the 18th Century." *Population Studies* 3: 3–65.

Golab, Caroline. 1973. "The Immigrant and the City: Poles, Italians, and Jews in Philadelphia, 1870–1920." In *The Peoples of Philadelphia: A History of Ethnic Groups and Lower-Class Life, 1790–1940,* edited by Allen F. Davis and Mark H. Haller, 203–30. Philadelphia.

Good, David F. 1974. "'Stagnation' and 'Take-Off' in Austria, 1873–1913." *Economic History Review* 27: 72–87.

———. 1984. *The Economic Rise of the Habsburg Empire, 1750–1914.* Berkeley.

Goubert, Pierre. 1960. *Beauvais et le Beauvaisis de 1600 à 1730; contribution à l'histoire de la France du xviie siècle.* 2 vols. Paris.

Grafenauer, Bogo. 1954–78. *Zgodovina slovenskega naroda* [The history of the Slovene people]. 5 vols. Ljubljana.

Gross, N. T. 1976. "The Hapsburg Monarchy, 1750–1914." In *The Fontana Economic History of Europe,* edited by Carlo M. Cipolla, vol. 4, pt. 1, 228–78. London.

Guldescu, Stanko. 1970. *The Croatian-Slavonian Kingdom 1526–1792.* Paris.

Gutman, Herbert. 1976. *Work, Culture and Society in Industrializing America: Essay in American Working-Class and Social History.* New York.

Halpern, Joel M. [1958] 1967. *A Serbian Village.* New York.

———. 1963. "Yugoslav Peasant Society in Transition—Stability in Change." *Anthropological Quarterly* 35: 156–82.

Hanagan, Michael P. 1980. *The Logic of Solidarity: Artisans and Industrial Workers in Three French Towns, 1871–1914.* Urbana, Ill.

Handlin, Oscar. 1951. *The Uprooted.* Boston.

Hareven, Tamara. 1981. *Family Time and Industrial Time: The Relationship between the Family and Work in a New England Industrial Community.* New York.

Held, Joseph, ed. 1980. *The Modernization of Agriculture: Rural Transformation in Hungary, 1848–1975.* Irvington, N.J.

Helleiner, Karl F. 1967. "The Population of Europe from the Black Death to the Eve of the Vital Revolution." In *The Cambridge Economic History of Europe,* edited by E. E. Rich and C. H. Wilson, vol. 3, 1–95. Cambridge, England.

Henige, David. 1982. *Oral Historiography.* London.

Herak, Milan, and V. T. Stringfield. 1972. *Karst: Important Karst Regions of the Northern Hemisphere.* Amsterdam, N.Y.

Hočevar, Toussaint. 1965. *The Structure of the Slovenian Economy, 1848–1963.* New York.

———. 1978. *The Economic History of Slovenia, 1828–1918: A Bibliography with Subject Index.* New York.

———. 1979. *Slovenski Družbeni Razvoj: Izbrana Razprave* [Slovene social development: Selected essays]. New Orleans.

Hoffman, Elizabeth [Newell]. 1981. *The Sources of Mortality Changes in Italy Since Unification.* New York.

Hohenberg, Paul M., and Lynn H. Lees. 1985. *The Making of Urban Europe, 1000–1950.* Cambridge, Mass.

Homans, George C. 1941. *English Villagers of the Thirteenth Century.* Cambridge, Mass.

———. 1950. *The Human Group.* New York.

Hughes, J. R. T., and Wilbert E. Moore. 1969. "Industrialization." *International Encyclopedia of the Social Sciences* 7: 252–70.

Hutchinson, Edward P. 1967. *The Population Debate: The Development of Conflicting Theories up to 1900.* Boston.

Italy. Istituto Centrale di Statistica. 1979. *Annuario statistico italiano.*

Kacin-Wohinz, Milica. 1972. *Primorski Slovenci pod italijansko zasedbo, 1918–21* [The coastland Slovenes under the Italian occupation, 1918–21]. Maribor, Yugoslavia.

———. 1977. *Narodnoobrambno gibanje primorskih Slovencev v letih 1921–28* [The movement of the coastland Slovenes in defense of their rights, 1918–28]. Koper, Yugoslavia.

Kann, Robert A. 1974. *A History of the Hapsburg Empire, 1526–1918.* Berkeley.

Katz, Friedrich. 1972. *The Ancient American Civilizations.* Translated by K. M. Lois Simpson. London.

Keene, Donald. 1952. *The Japanese Discovery of Europe.* London.

Kessinger, Tom G. 1974. *Vilyatpur, 1848–1968: Social and Economic Change in a North Indian Village.* Berkeley.

Knodel, John E. 1974. *The Decline of Fertility in Germany, 1871–1939.* Princeton.

Kochanowicz, Jacek. 1983. "The Peasant Family as an Economic Unit in the Polish Feudal Economy of the Eighteenth Century." In *Family Forms in Historic Europe,* edited by Richard Wall, 153–66. Cambridge, England.

Kos, Milko. 1939–54. *Srednjeveški urbarji za Slovenijo* [Medieval Slovene charter books]. 3 vols. Ljubljana.

Kos, Milko, Lavo Čermelj, Bogo Grafenauer, et al. 1974. *The Slovenes in Italy Yesterday and Today.* Translated by Franc Slivnik. Trieste.

Lampe, John R., and Marvin R. Jackson. 1982. *Balkan Imperial History, 1550–1950: From Imperial Borderlands to Developing Nations.* Bloomington, Ind.

Landes, David S. 1969. *The Unbound Prometheus: Technological Change and Industrial Development in Western Europe from 1750 to the Present.* London.

Langer, William L. 1963. "Europe's Initial Population Explosion." *American Historical Review* 69: 1–17.

Laslett, Peter. 1972. "Mean Household Size in England Since the Sixteenth Century." In *Household and Family in Past Time,* edited by Peter Laslett and Richard Wall, 125–58. Cambridge, England.

Latrobe, Charles J. 1832. *The Pedestrian: A Summer's Ramble in the Tyrol, and Some of the Adjacent Provinces MDCCCXXX.* London.

Lees, Lynn H. 1979. *Exiles of Erin: Irish Immigrants in Victorian London.* Ithaca, N.Y.

Lehning, James R. 1980. *The Peasants of Marlhes: Economic Development and Family Organization in 19th Century France.* Chapel Hill, N.C.

Lenček, Rado L. 1947. "Od Tržiča do Trsta" [From Monfalcone to Trieste]. *Ob Jadranu: Etnografski zapiski in študije* [Along the Adriatic: Ethnographic notes and studies], 61–62. Trieste.

Lerner, Gerda. 1971. *The Woman in American History.* Menlo Park, Calif.

Le Roy Ladurie, Emmanuel. 1974. *The Peasants of Languedoc.* Translated by John Day. Urbana, Ill.

———. 1979. *Montaillou The Promised Land of Error.* Translated by Barbara Bray. New York.

Lesthaeghe, Ron J. 1977. *The Decline of Belgian Fertility.* Princeton.

Livi Bacci, Massimo. 1971. *A Century of Portuguese Fertility.* Princeton.

———. 1977. *A History of Italian Fertility during the Last Two Centuries.* Princeton.

Lockwood, William G. 1976. "The Peasant-Worker in Yugoslavia." In *The Social Structure of Eastern Europe,* edited by Bernard L. Faber, 281–300. New York.

Lokar, Aleš. 1977. "Posizione economica e sociale della popolazione slovena a Trieste e Gorizia nel periodo precedente la prima guerra mondiale e l'opera di Henrik

Tuma." *Prispevki za zgodovino delavskega* [Contributions to the history of labor] 17: nos. 1–2. Ljubljana.

Lokar, Aleš, and Lee Thomas. 1977. "Socioeconomic Structure of the Slovene Population in Italy." *Papers in Slovene Studies,* 26–39.

Lokar, Aleš. 1983. "The Impact of Technological Change on a Bilingual Community: The Case of Duino-Aurisina/Devin-Nabrežina, Italy." Pp. 162–74 in Davis, Pirjevec, Lokar, and Sussi, "Symposium: The Slovenes of Northeastern Italy," *Nationalites Papers* 11 (1983): 148–89.

Lokar, Aleš, and Marco J. Oblak. 1983. "Adaptation to Change and Innovation in a Bilingual Community." Paper presented at the Second International Congress on Minority Languages, Turku-Abo, Finland.

Lucas, Henry S. 1930. "The Great European Famine of 1315, 1316, 1317." *Speculum* 5: 343–77.

Lutyens, Mary, ed. 1965. *Effie in Venice. Unpublished Letters of Mrs. John Ruskin written from Venice between 1849–1852.* London.

Luzzatto Fegiz, Pierpaolo. 1929. *La popolazione di Trieste (1875–1928).* Trieste.

Macartney, Carile A. 1968. *The Hapsburg Empire, 1790–1918.* London.

McKeown, Thomas. 1976. *The Modern Rise of Population.* London.

Malthus, Thomas R. [1798] 1926. *An Essay on the Principle of Population.* London.

Marwick, Arthur. 1974. *War and Social Change in the Twentieth Century: A Comparative Study of Britain, France, Germany, Russia and the United States.* London.

Marx, Karl, and Friedrich Engels. [1848] 1967. *The Communist Manifesto.* New York.

Matis, Herbert, and Karl Bachinger. 1973. "Österreichs industrielle Entwicklung." In *Die Habsburger Monarchie 1848–1918,* edited by Alois Brusatti, 105–232. Vienna.

Matthiessen, Poul C., and James C. McCann. 1978. "The Role of Mortality in the European Fertility Transition: Aggregate-Level Relations." In *The Effects of Infant and Child Mortality on Fertility,* edited by Samuel H. Preston. New York.

Melograni, Piero. 1972. *Gli industriali e Mussolini. Rapporti tra Confindustria e fascismo dal 1919 al 1929.* Milan.

Mendels, Franklin. 1972. "Protoindustrialization: The First Phase of the Industrialization Process." *Journal of Economic History* 32: 241–61.

Merkù, Pavle. 1976. *Ljudsko izročilo Slovencev v Italiji zbrano v letih 1965–1974* [Ethnic heritage of the Slovenes in Italy collected during 1965–1974]. Trieste.

Mervic-Legiša, Zorka, and Dušan Furlan. 1970. *Občina Devin-Nabrežina v boju proti Nacifašizmu* [Duino-Nabrežina township in the struggle against Nazism-Fascism]. Trieste.

Mihelič, Dušan. 1969. *The Political Element in the Port Geography of Trieste.* Chicago.

Milward, Alan. 1977. *War, Economy and Society: 1939–1945.* Berkeley.

Minchinton, Walter. 1973. "Patterns of Demand 1750–1914." In *The Fontana Economic History of Europe,* edited by Carlo M. Cipolla, vol. 3, 77–186. London.

Minnich, Robert. 1979. *The Homemade World of Zagaj: An Interpretation of the 'Practical Life' among Traditional Peasant-Farmers in West-Holoze, Slovenia, Yugoslavia.* Bergen.

Molek, Ivan. [1932] 1978. *Two Worlds.* Translated by Mary Molek. Dover, Del.

Montanelli, Pietro. 1905. *Il movimento storico della popolazione di Trieste.* Trieste.

Moritsch, Andreas. 1969. *Das nahe Triester Hinterland. Zur wirtschaftlichen und sozialen Entwicklung vom Beginn des 19. Jahrhunderts bis zur Gegenwart.* Vienna.

Nacci, Franco, ed. 1963. *Enciclopedia dei comuni d'Italia: Trieste e la provincia.* Rome.

Nasti, Agostino. 1934. *Movimento operaio e socialismo.* Milan.

Nice, Bruno. 1940. *La casa rurale nella Venezia Giulia.* Bologna.

Novak, Bogdan C. 1970. *Trieste 1941–1954: The Ethnic, Political and Ideological Struggle.* Chicago.

Österreichisches Recht. 1968–71. 3 vols. Vol. 1, *Allgemeines Burgerliches Gesetzbuch.* Vienna.

Österreichisch-ungarische Monarchie in Wort und Bild, Die. 1891. Vol. 10, *Das Küstenlande.* Vienna.

Overbeek, Hans. 1970. "Un démographe prémalthusien au xviiie siècle: Giammaria Ortes." *Population* 25: 563–71.

Ožbalt, Marija A. I. 1981. "The Theme of the Unwed Mother in Slovene Literature." *Slovene Studies* 3: 59–71.

Pagnini, Cesare, ed. 1952. "Un viaggio del luglio 1800 nella Venezia Giulia." *Archeografo triestino* 18–19: 21–37.

Pagnini, Maria Paola. 1966. *La casa rurale del Carso triestino.* Trieste.

Paton, A. A. 1849. *Highlands and Islands of the Adriatic.* 2 vols. London.

Peters, H. Frederick. 1960. *Rainer Maria Rilke: Masks and the Man.* Seattle.

Pichler, Rodolfo. 1882. *Il castello di Duino. Memorie.* Trento.

Pirjevec, Jože. 1983a. "Slovene Nationalism in Trieste, 1848–1982." Pp. 152–61 in Davis, Pirjevec, Lokar, and Sussi, "Symposium: The Slovenes of Northeastern Italy," *Nationalities Papers* 11 (1983): 148–89.

Pollard, Sidney. 1963. "Factory Discipline in the Industrial Revolution." *Economic History Review* 16: 254–71.

———. 1981. *Peaceful Conquest: The Industrialization of Europe, 1790–1970.* Oxford.

Post, J. D. 1976. "Famine, Mortality and Epidemic Disease in the Process of Modernization." *Economic History Review* 29: 14–37.

Postan, Michael M. 1967. *An Economic History of Western Europe, 1945–1964.* London.

Potter, Jack M., May N. Diaz, and George M. Foster. 1967. *Peasant Society: A Reader.* Boston.

Preston, Samuel H., and Étienne van de Walle. 1978. "Urban French Mortality in the Nineteenth Century." *Population Studies* 32: 275–97.

Prude, Jonathan. 1983. *The Coming of Industrial Order: Town and Factory Life in Rural Massachusetts 1810–1860.* Cambridge, England.

Rilke, Rainer Maria. 1939. *Duino Elegies.* Edited and translated by J. B. Leishman and Stephen Spender. New York.

———. 1958. *The Letters of Rainer Maria Rilke and Princess Maria von Thurn und Taxis.* Translated by Nora Wydenbruck. Norfolk, Conn.

Rogers, Everett M. 1969. *Modernization Among Peasants: The Impact of Communication.* New York.

Rowntree, B. Seebohm. 1922. *Poverty, A Study of Town Life.* London.

Ruatti, G. 1934. "Le proprietà consortili del Carso con speciale riguardo a Castelnuovo d'Istria." *La Porta Orientale,* vol. 3, issue 3/4: 191–234.

Rusinow, Dennison I. 1969. *Italy's Austrian Heritage, 1919–1946.* Oxford.

Schmid, Abramo. 1977. "Sul Carso della Grande Guerra: Medeazza—Note di escursioni e ricerche." *Alpi Giulie* 71: 33–67.

Scott, Joan W., and Louise A. Tilly. 1975. "Women's Work and the Family in Nineteenth-Century Europe." *Comparative Studies in Society and History* 17: 36–64.

Semerani, Luciano, Diana de Rosa, and Luciano Celli. 1970. *Il Carso triestino: Santa Croce.* Trieste.

Shorter, Edward. 1975. *The Making of the Modern Family.* New York.

———. 1982. *A History of Women's Bodies.* New York.

Shoumatoff, Alex. 1985. "The Mountain of Names." *The New Yorker*, 13 May: 51–101.

Silberman, Leo. 1959–60. "Hung Liang-Chi: a Chinese Malthus." *Population Studies* 13: 257–65.

Slicher van Bath, Bernard H. 1963. *The Agrarian History of Western Europe*, A.D. 500–1850. Translated by Olive Ordish. London.

———. 1967. "Agriculture in the Vital Revolution." In *The Cambridge Economic History of Europe*, edited by E. E. Rich and C. H. Wilson, vol. 4, 42–132. Cambridge, England.

Società Alpina delle Giulie, ed. 1909. *Guida dei dintorni di Trieste*. Trieste.

Sokoloff, Kenneth L., and Giorgia C. Villaflor. 1982. "The Early Achievement of Modern Stature in America." *Social Science History* 6: 453–81.

Spengler, Joseph J. 1942. *French Predecessors of Malthus*. Durham, N.C.

Stearns, Peter N. 1975. *European Society in Upheaval: Social History Since 1750*. 2d ed. New York.

Strakosch, Henry C. 1967. *State Absolutism and the Rule of Law. The Struggle for the Codification of Civil Law in Austria, 1753–1811*. Sydney.

Susel, Rudolph M. 1977. "Aspects of the Slovene Community in Cleveland, Ohio." *Papers in Slovene Studies 1977*, 64–72.

Sussi, Emidio. 1983. "Psycho-Sociological Aspects of Relations among Three Ethnic Groups: Slovenes, Italians and Friulians." Pp. 176–85 in Davis, Pirjevec, Lokar, and Sussi, "Symposium: The Slovenes of Northeastern Italy," *Nationalities Papers* 11 (1983): 148–89.

Sweden. Statistike central Byran. 1969–72. *Historik statistik för Sverige*. 2d ed., pt. 1. Stockholm.

Sweeting, Marjorie Mary. 1973. *Karst Landforms*. New York.

Tamaro, Attilio. 1924. *Storia di Trieste*. 2 vols. Rome.

Thernstrom, Stephan. 1964. *Poverty and Progress: Social Mobility in a Nineteenth Century City*. Cambridge, Mass.

Thomas, Keith. 1964 . "Work and Leisure in a Pre-Industrial Society." *Past and Present* 29: 50–62.

Thomas, William I., and Florian Znaniecki. 1918–20. *The Polish Peasant in Europe and America*. 4 vols. Chicago.

Thompson, E. P. 1967. "Time, Work-Discipline, and Industrial Capitalism." *Past and Present* 38: 56–97.

Tilly, Charles, ed. 1978. *Historical Studies of Changing Fertility*. New York.

Tilly, Louise A., and Joan W. Scott. 1978. *Women, Work and Family*. New York.

Trebilcock, Clive. 1981. *The Industrialization of the Continental Powers, 1780–1914*. New York.

Vinovskis, Maris A. 1977. "From Household Size to the Life Course. Some Observations on Recent Trends in Family History." *American Behaviorial Scientist* 21: 263–87.

Vivante, Angelo. [1912] 1945. *Irredentismo adriatico. Contributo alla discussione sui rapporti austro-italiani*. Trieste.

Wall, Richard, ed. 1983. *Family Forms in Historic Europe*. Cambridge, England.

Warriner, Doreen, ed. 1965. *Contrasts in Emerging Societies. Readings in the Social and Economic History of South Central Europe*. Bloomington, Ind.

Weber, Adna. [1899] 1969. *The Growth of Cities in the 19th Century: A Study in Statistics*. New York.

Williams, Robert H. 1968. *Textbook of Endocrinology*. 4th ed. Philadelphia.

Winner, Irene P. 1971. *A Slovenian Village: Žerovnica*. Providence, R.I.

————. 1977a. "Ethnicity among Urban Slovene Villagers in Cleveland, Ohio." *Papers in Slovene Studies 1977,* 51–63.

————. 1977b. "The Question of Cultural Point of View in Determining the Boundaries of Ethnic Units: Slovene Villagers in the Cleveland, Ohio Area." *Papers in Slovene Studies 1977,* 73–82.

————. 1977c. "The Question of the Zadruga in Slovenia: Myth and Reality in Žerovnica." *Anthropological Quarterly* 50: 125–34.

Wolf, Eric R. 1963. "Kinship, Friendship and Patron-Client Relations in Complex Societies." In *The Social Anthropology of Complex Societies,* edited by Michael Banton, 1–22. London.

Wolff, Robert. 1956. *The Balkans in Our Time.* Cambridge, Mass.

Wylie, Laurence W. 1966. *Chanzeaux, A Village in Anjou.* Cambridge, Mass.

Zinsser, Hans. 1960. *Rats, Lice and History.* New York.

Žužek, Patrizia. 1983–84. "Lo sviluppo delle scuole e l'attività associativa slovena nel comune di Duino-Aurisina tra il xviii° e il xx° secolo." Laurea thesis, University of Trieste.

Index

agriculture. *See* farming
alcohol. *See* drinking, wine
amusements. *See* leisure
Austria (and Austria-Hungary), 6, 14–15, 31–32, 37, 87, 92–93

barns, 16, 47, 52, 56
beds, 17, 108
beggars, 75, 111, 130
birth control, 99–101
birth rates. *See* fertility
breast-feeding, 24–25, 100

Cankar, Ivan, 80–81
carting, 36, 42, 45–46, 68, 82
caste, 34
cattle, 17, 19–21, 28–29, 35, 38, 41, 47, 53, 56, 72–73, 122
children, 29, 41, 49, 51, 101–04, 108–09
church registers, xv
citizenship, 34, 70
climate, 4, 7–8, 19, 21
clothing, 16–17, 26, 39, 49, 52, 57, 117–18, 130
colonization, 11
common, village, 18
courts, 18
crime, 62, 81, 95
crops. *See* grains, haying, potatoes, vegetables

daughters, 9–10, 53–55, 104
death rate. *See* mortality
deference, 29, 102
deforestation, 4
dental care. *See* teeth
diarrhea. *See* dysentery
diet, xiii, 7, 9, 16, 39–41, 48, 51–52, 89, 96, 108
discipline: family, 29, 101–02, 142 n.4; industrial, 45, 89, 121; military, 85
disease, 9, 11, 14–15, 22–23, 25–26, 50, 52–53, 66, 89, 110, 122, 127. *See also* diarrhea, dysentery, puerperal fever, smallpox, tuberculosis, typhus
doctors. *See* medicine
domestic service, 56, 102–04
dowry, 55, 67
drinking, 80, 82, 90. *See also* wine
dues to lord, 10, 12–13, 15, 18, 20, 22, 26, 28, 31, 33, 48
Duino castle and fief, xii, xv, 5–6, 32–35; map, 5
dung, 20, 53, 110
dysentery, 23, 25–26, 39, 52, 66

earth. *See* soil
education, xiii, 17, 62, 70–71, 90, 92, 102–05, 109, 117
elderly: care of, 17, 24, 49–50, 127, 130

emancipation, 14–15, 27–28, 42–43
employment. *See* domestic service, farming, milkmaids, quarrying, sardines, service sector, shipyards

family structure, 9, 29, 46, 101–02, 142 n.4
family tree, xiv. *See also* list of tables, x; line of descent (table), xiv
famine, 15, 21–22
farming, xi, xiii, 12, 18, 20–21, 26, 28–29, 38–46, 52, 70, 72, 83, 151 n.9
fertility, 17, 23–26, 99–101, 134
first night: right of. *See* right of first night
fishing, 55, 59
flies, 23, 122
folk songs, 26 n, 40, 138 n.5
food: quantity of, 14, 16, 23, 48–49, 51–52, 112, 117, 130
fortresses, 5–6, 9, 11, 64, 137 n.36
Francis Joseph I (Emperor), 32, 86
fuel, 4, 26, 97
furnishings of houses, 17, 108, 116

genealogy. *See* list of tables, x
ghetto (Slovene), 60
grains, 7, 40
graves, 130–32

hamlets, xi, 10, 16, 84
Hapsburgs, 6, 9, 31–32, 86. *See also* Austria (and Austria-Hungary)
hauling. *See* carting
haying, 40–41, 45, 59
height, 16, 44, 139 n.11
heiresses: peasant, 16, 55
hereditary subjection, 31–32
housing, xiii, 7, 19, 24, 47–48, 51–53, 84, 108, 116–17, 125, 127
hunting, 4, 8, 11, 95–96
hygiene, 23, 51–53, 63

illegitimacy, 81
illustrations: list of, ix
industrialization, xi, xiii, 31, 36, 42–50, 54, 72, 79, 82, 90, 92–93, 104–05, 117
infant mortality. *See* mortality
inheritance, 7, 9–10, 12–14, 29, 60, 66–68, 77, 101, 128
Italianization, 92, 102–03
"Italian miracle," 120–21, 124
Italy, 84–87, 91–93, 103, 107, 112, 120–22; map, xii

Joseph II (Holy Roman Emperor), 14–15

Karst plateau, xi–xiii, 3–5, 16, 87, 120, 135 n.2; maps, xii, 5
kinship, 13, 15

labor camps, 113–16
labor services to lord, 6, 8, 10, 15, 31, 33
labor supply, 28–29, 65
labor: division of, 24–25, 29, 36, 40–41, 45–46, 49, 96–97, 102–03
land, 3–4, 12–14, 33, 38, 134, 135 n.1
language. *See* Italianization, Slovene language
legal system, 18
Le Roy Ladurie, Emmanuel, 3, 20
lice, 110, 148 n.12
line of descent (table), xiv. *See also* list of tables, x
literacy, 70–71, 77, 101
living standard. *See* standard of living
lottery, 125
love, 15, 55, 59, 138–39 n.5

Malthus, Thomas, 3, 14
manpower. *See* labor supply
manure, 20, 53, 110
maps: list of, ix
Marija: use of as name, 141 n.46
marriage, 10, 12, 15, 24–25, 28, 33, 53–63, 68, 74, 88–90, 126
medicine, xiii, 51, 53, 109–10, 117, 122, 130
midwives, 23, 53
military service, 11, 34, 62, 68, 81, 83
milkmaids, 20, 39, 55, 57, 88–89
modernization, xi, 36, 91, 96–97, 104–06
mortality, 15, 22–26, 39, 51–54, 77, 90, 99, 110, 134
myth, 32–33

Napoleonic wars, 20–22
niche, 4, 10–13, 27
nicknames, 11, 29, 60, 76
old age. *See* elderly: care of
Old Order, 27, 29, 54

partisans, 112–19
patriotism, 85–86
pay, 91
peasants, xv, 69–70, 77–78
personality, 29, 46, 54–56, 63, 68, 74–77, 80, 91

population, 37, 57, 77
potatoes, 40, 52, 143 n.11, 145 n.3
priests, 17, 59, 148 n.3
primogeniture. *See* inheritance
proletariat, 78–79, 90
pronunciation of Slovene names, xii (note)
prosperity of 1950s and 1960s, 92, 102–03
public services, 73, 109
puerperal fever, 23, 53

quarrying, 4, 42–43, 46, 52, 82–83, 91, 94, 120

railroad, 36, 42–43, 64, 73, 94–95
rebellions: peasant, 6 n, 31, 33
registers: church, xv
religion. *See* priests, worship
rent. *See* dues to lord
Revolution of 1848, 31–32
right of the first night, 32–33, 142 n.11
Rilke, Rainer Maria, 31 n, 89 n
roads, 18, 42, 57, 87, 109, 120, 122, 128
Ruskin, Euphemia, 34–35

sanitation. *See* hygiene
sardines, 89
school. *See* education
serfdom, xii–xiii, 3, 6–7, 10–11, 14–15, 26, 31–32, 134, 136 n.11
servants. *See* domestic service
service sector, 121, 124
sheep, 17, 19–20, 38–39, 42, 52
shipyards, 83, 121
silkworms, 41–43, 88–89
Slavs, xi. *See also* Slovenes
Slivno, 7
slivovitz, 7
Slovene language, xi, 4, 43, 91–93, 123, 128
Slovenes, xi, 4, 43, 91–93, 123, 128
smallpox, 15, 39, 53
soccer lottery, 125
social mobility, 35, 59 n
soil, 18, 21, 24, 26
sources, xiii–xiv
standard of living, 9, 16–17, 26, 46–49, 77, 94–95, 100, 107–12, 121
stature. *See* height
subsistence farming. *See* farming
suburbanization, 120, 122–23. *See also* urbanization
surplusa people, 53–63, 66, 90

tables, list of, x
taxes, 20, 34
teeth, 109, 130
testament, 24, 66
Torre e Tasso, della, xv, 6 n, 15, 21–22, 28, 32–35, 110–111, 128 143 n.16
transportation, 41, 83, 109, 117, 122, 124, 130
trees, 4–5, 11, 16
Trieste, xi, 4, 31, 36–39, 43, 60, 72–73, 87, 92, 100, 123–24
tuberculosis, 22–23, 25–26, 53, 66, 74, 110, 130
Turks, 9, 11
typhus, 53, 89, 148 n.12

unions, 121
urbanization, 36, 60, 77, 79, 124. *See also* suburbanization

vegetables, 96–97, 108
Vižovlje, 10–13, 16, 63–65, 87, 94, 112–16; map, 19
voting. *See* citizenship

walking, 41, 57, 89 n, 123–24
want, xi–xiii. *See also* standard of living
water, 7, 23, 41, 48, 51–52, 94, 97, 109
wealth of Žužeks, xi–xiii, 9, 21, 33, 38, 77, *See also* standard of living
will, 24, 66
windows, 48, 52–53
wine, 11, 40, 48, 62
wood (fuel), 4, 26, 97
women. *See* daughters, dowry, family, heiresses, labor: division of, marriage, midwives, milkmaids
wool, 20, 39, 42, 49, 118. *See also* sheep
work, 20–21, 40, 71, 76, 87, 93–94, 98–99, 104, 121, 123–26, 130, 140 n26. *See also* employment; labor, division of
World War I, 81, 84–87, 89
World War II, 77, 107–8, 112–20
worms, 39, 53
worship, 26, 41, 48, 109–11, 131

Yugoslavia, xi, 120; map, xii

zadruga, 138 n40
Žužek, passim